Phonics and Vocabulary Skills Practice and Apply: Grade 5

BY
MYRL SHIREMAN

ISBN 1-58037-132-9

Printing No. CD-1354

Mark Twain Media, Inc., Publishers
Distributed by Carson-Dellosa Publishing Company, Inc.

Table of Contents

Table of Contents

Table of Contents

Introduction

This book for Grade Five is one of a phonics and vocabulary series that also includes Grade Four and Grade Six. In Grade Four the basic sight words needed for each exercise were highlighted. In this Grade Five book, it is assumed that students have mastered many of the basic sight words needed to complete each exercise. Activities in this book are designed to give students ample opportunity to review and extend skills learned in Grade Four and be introduced to new skills.

In many of the activities, the student is required to write sentences to apply the skills learned. This is an important aspect of the book intended to insure that the student understands and can apply the given skill. When students demonstrate that they can compose sentences using the skill, it is more likely that the skill will be retained and used accurately in classroom reading situations.

Periodically an activity will appear to be out of sequence and unrelated to the skills in a particular section. These apparently unrelated activities are designed to aid the student in maintaining the phonics skills learned in prior activities.

Name: ______________________________ Date: ____________________

Learning to Use the Dictionary: *Using Guide Words to Locate Words*

At the top of each page of a dictionary you will find **guide words**. The guide words are the first and last words that will be found on a page in a dictionary. The first guide word is found on the top left of the page, and the last word is found at the bottom right of the page.

Guide Words
Example: collar/color

1. Use a dictionary and complete the following for selected pages in that dictionary.

   Title of Dictionary: ______________________________

Page #	First Guide Word on Page	Last Guide Word on Page
______	______________________	______________________
______	______________________	______________________
______	______________________	______________________
______	______________________	______________________
______	______________________	______________________
______	______________________	______________________
______	______________________	______________________
______	______________________	______________________
______	______________________	______________________
______	______________________	______________________

2. Choose a page in the dictionary. Write the guide words found on the page in the blanks below. Then write all the words found on the page between those guide words on the lines below.

   Guide Word Top Left: ____________ **Guide Word Bottom Right:** ____________

________________	________________	________________
________________	________________	________________
________________	________________	________________
________________	________________	________________
________________	________________	________________
________________	________________	________________
________________	________________	________________

Name: ______________________________ Date: ____________________

Learning to Use the Dictionary: *Learning to Use the Pronunciation Guide*

Many times you will need to use the dictionary to pronounce an unknown word. To use the dictionary, you must understand the symbols used for the phonetic spellings of words.

1. Select a dictionary and turn to the page labeled **Guide to Pronunciation**. Using the Guide to Pronunciation, complete the following.

Letter(s)	Sound of Letter	Letter + Symbol	Example Words	
a	long sound	_____	__________	__________
a	short sound	_____	__________	__________
e	long sound	_____	__________	__________
e	short sound	_____	__________	__________
i	long sound	_____	__________	__________
i	short sound	_____	__________	__________
o	long sound	_____	__________	__________
o	short sound	_____	__________	__________
u	long sound	_____	__________	__________
u	short sound	_____	__________	__________

2. Find the following words in the dictionary. Complete the blanks, showing the phonetic spelling for each word.

	Word	Phonetic Spelling
a.	huge	____________________
b.	machine	____________________
c.	dismay	____________________
d.	brain	____________________
e.	galosh	____________________
f.	primer	____________________
g.	system	____________________
h.	hustle	____________________
i.	depot	____________________
j.	crust	____________________

Name: ______________________ Date: ______________________

Learning to Use Vowels

Complete the blanks in the following sentences using the vowels at the end of each sentence. Indicate the long vowel sound by placing the macron symbol (¯) over the vowel. Indicate the short vowel sound by placing the breve symbol (˘) over the vowel. Indicate a silent vowel with the slash (/) through the vowel letter.

1. The m___ n sat by the s___d___ of the r___ ___d looking very s___d. **e a o i**
2. They sw___m the w___d___ river with ___ase. **i e a**
3. I will b___ on t___m___. **i e**
4. D___d you see the f___n___ m___l___ sh___ was riding? **e i u**
5. She was gr___t___ful for the r___d___ on the b___k___. **i e a**
6. When d___ you th___nk the pl___n___ will l___nd? **i o a e**
7. H___ will play the l___t___, and I will play the fl___t___. **u e**
8. The bl___ck r___t in the c___g___ was f___t. **a e**
9. H___ played the t___n___ with ___as___. **u e**
10. I ___m very sad th___t you d___d n___t find the cl___ck. **i a o**
11. The k___ttl___ has a l___ttl___ h___ndl___. **a e i**
12. The p___cn___c b___sk___t was f___ll of food. **a e i u**

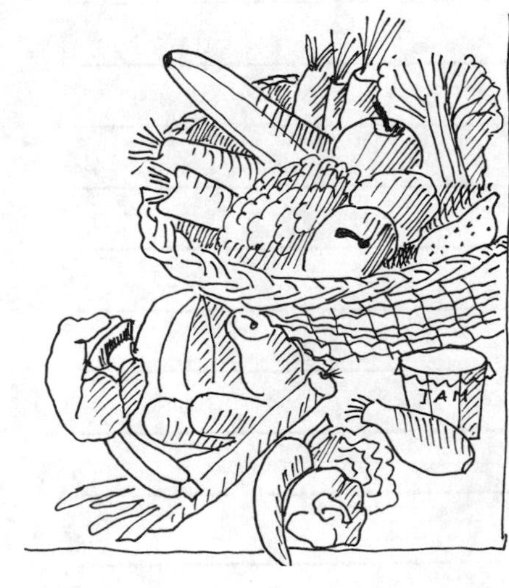

Name: ______________________________ Date: ____________________

Learning to Use Vowels: *Learning About Long and Short Vowel Sounds*

When a vowel sound is the long sound, the vowel is the name of the vowel.

Example: The vowel "i" is long in the word "bite." In the dictionary, the long sound of a vowel is shown with the macron (¯) placed over the vowel with the long sound.

The short sound of the vowel "i" is the sound heard in the word "bit." Pronounce the words out loud to hear the difference between the long and short sounds of the letter "i." Note the use of the macron (¯) and breve (˘) to mark the long and short sounds of the vowel.

long sound = bīte **short sound = bĭt**

Each of the following words has a long or short vowel sound. Place the words with the long vowel sound in the Long Vowel Sound column. Place the words with the short vowel sound in the Short Vowel Sound column.

dime	**rip**	**tape**	**hat**	**robe**	**tube**
mate	**pin**	**huge**	**note**	**tap**	**ripe**
hate	**pine**	**hug**	**tub**	**dim**	**rob**
not	**mat**				

	Long Vowel Sound	**Short Vowel Sound**
1.	____________	____________
2.	____________	____________
3.	____________	____________
4.	____________	____________
5.	____________	____________
6.	____________	____________
7.	____________	____________
8.	____________	____________
9.	____________	____________
10.	____________	____________

Name: ______________________ Date: ______________

Learning About Silent "e": *Understanding the Long Vowel-Consonant-Silent "e" Pattern*

In many words the final "e" is silent. For example, "bike" is pronounced with a long "i" and silent "e." In Column I is a word. Pronounce the word and complete the blanks. In Column II place the letter "e" on the blank to make a word. Pronounce the new word and complete the blanks. Write a sentence using both words.

Column I	Vowel Sound long/short/silent	Column II	Vowel Sounds long/short/silent
1. **not**	________	not__	________
Sentence: ________			
2. **bit**	________	bit__	________
Sentence: ________			
3. **rat**	________	rat__	________
Sentence: ________			
4. **fat**	________	fat__	________
Sentence: ________			
5. **hat**	________	hat__	________
Sentence: ________			
6. **cut**	________	cut__	________
Sentence: ________			
7. **pin**	________	pin__	________
Sentence: ________			
8. **pan**	________	pan__	________
Sentence: ________			
9. **man**	________	man__	________
Sentence: ________			
10. **fin**	________	fin__	________
Sentence: ________			
11. **ton**	________	ton__	________
Sentence: ________			
12. **met**	________	met__	________
Sentence: ________			

Name: ______________________________ Date: ____________________

Learning About Silent "e": *Using Words With Silent "e"*

Each of the words below has a long vowel sound with a silent "e." Rewrite the word and place a macron (¯) over the vowel that is long and draw a slash (/) through the silent "e." Use a dictionary to determine the meaning of each word. Pronounce each word and write a sentence using the word.

1. **tune** ___ ___ ___ ___
   Meaning: ______________________________
   Sentence: ______________________________
2. **rile** ___ ___ ___ ___
   Meaning: ______________________________
   Sentence: ______________________________
3. **base** ___ ___ ___ ___
   Meaning: ______________________________
   Sentence: ______________________________
4. **fuse** ___ ___ ___ ___
   Meaning: ______________________________
   Sentence: ______________________________
5. **bile** ___ ___ ___ ___
   Meaning: ______________________________
   Sentence: ______________________________
6. **sage** ___ ___ ___ ___
   Meaning: ______________________________
   Sentence: ______________________________
7. **dote** ___ ___ ___ ___
   Meaning: ______________________________
   Sentence: ______________________________
8. **rote** ___ ___ ___ ___
   Meaning: ______________________________
   Sentence: ______________________________
9. **rife** ___ ___ ___ ___
   Meaning: ______________________________
   Sentence: ______________________________

Name: ______________________ Date: ______________

Learning About Silent "e": *Using Words With Silent "e"*

Each of the words below has a long vowel sound with a silent "e." Rewrite the word and place a macron (¯) over the vowel that is long and draw a slash (/) through the silent "e." Use a dictionary to determine the meaning of each word. Pronounce each word and write a sentence using the word.

1. **dupe** ___ ___ ___ ___
   Meaning: ______________________
   Sentence: ______________________
2. **mope** ___ ___ ___ ___
   Meaning: ______________________
   Sentence: ______________________
3. **wade** ___ ___ ___ ___
   Meaning: ______________________
   Sentence: ______________________
4. **mite** ___ ___ ___ ___
   Meaning: ______________________
   Sentence: ______________________
5. **bale** ___ ___ ___ ___
   Meaning: ______________________
   Sentence: ______________________
6. **mute** ___ ___ ___ ___
   Meaning: ______________________
   Sentence: ______________________
7. **cape** ___ ___ ___ ___
   Meaning: ______________________
   Sentence: ______________________
8. **rave** ___ ___ ___ ___
   Meaning: ______________________
   Sentence: ______________________
9. **yule** ___ ___ ___ ___
   Meaning: ______________________
   Sentence: ______________________

Name: ______________________________ Date: ____________________

Learning About Silent "e": *Using Words With Silent "e"*

Each of the words below has a long vowel sound with a silent "e." Rewrite the word and place a macron (¯) over the vowel that is long and draw a slash (/) through the silent "e." Use a dictionary to determine the meaning of each word. Pronounce each word and write a sentence using the word.

1. **tote** ___ ___ ___ ___
   Meaning: ______________________________
   Sentence: ______________________________
2. **mete** ___ ___ ___ ___
   Meaning: ______________________________
   Sentence: ______________________________
3. **hale** ___ ___ ___ ___
   Meaning: ______________________________
   Sentence: ______________________________
4. **pose** ___ ___ ___ ___
   Meaning: ______________________________
   Sentence: ______________________________
5. **rule** ___ ___ ___ ___
   Meaning: ______________________________
   Sentence: ______________________________
6. **brute** ___ ___ ___ ___ ___
   Meaning: ______________________________
   Sentence: ______________________________
7. **rime** ___ ___ ___ ___
   Meaning: ______________________________
   Sentence: ______________________________
8. **mote** ___ ___ ___ ___
   Meaning: ______________________________
   Sentence: ______________________________
9. **pace** ___ ___ ___ ___
   Meaning: ______________________________
   Sentence: ______________________________

Name: ______________________________ Date: ______________

Learning About Silent "e": *More Practice With Silent "e"*

Each of the following sentences contains a word with a long vowel and a silent "e" at the end. Find the word and write it on the blank following the sentence. Mark the word using the macron (¯) and slash (/) to show the correct punctuation. On the blank below the sentence, tell what the word means in the sentence.

1. His gaze told me that he was thinking of times long ago. ______________

   ____

2. A small boat is unsteady in a strong gale. ______________

   ____

3. The fume from the smokestack caused our eyes to water. ______________

   ____

4. The deer in the glade was eating peacefully. ______________

   ____

5. The jibe from the bullies was ignored. ______________

   ____

6. Emily's family is from a shire in England. ______________

   ____

7. They tried to dupe us into paying the bill. ______________

   ____

8. His grave look told us the problem was real. ______________

   ____

9. His pace increased at the end of the 100-meter dash. ______________

   ____

10. Everyone was quiet as we approached the shrine. ______________

    ____

11. She sat mute after reading the letter. ______________

    ____

12. In the old days, every barber had a hone. ______________

    ____

Name: ______________________________ Date: ____________________

Learning About Silent "e": *Sentence Completion Using Silent "e" Words*

Use the bold words below to complete the following sentences. Choose the dictionary phonetic spelling of the word from the list on the right. Write the spelling chosen on the blank under Dictionary Phonetic Spelling.

tile wade bone cake lone yule rule mule safe fine

	Dictionary Phonetic Spelling	
1. I rode the ______________.	______________	**wād**
2. Do you feel ______________?	______________	**tīl**
3. The dog chewed on the ______________ .	______________	**fīn**
4. They plan to ______________ in the water.	______________	**bōn**
5. He broke the ______________.	______________	**ūl**
6. Christmas is the ______________ season.	______________	**rūl**
7. The floor is made of ______________.	______________	**lōn**
8. Did you eat the birthday ______________?	______________	**sāf**
9. Sarah said she was feeling ______________.	______________	**mūl**
10. We heard a ______________ wolf in the hills.	______________	**cāk**

Name: ______________________________ Date: ____________________

Learning About Silent "e": *More Practice Using Silent "e"*

Write the correct pronunciation of each of the following words on the dashed lines, placing the macron (¯) over the vowels with the long sound and a slash (/) through silent letters. Write the dictionary spelling of the word on the blank. Then write the meaning of the word on the blank. Finally, use each of the words to make a sentence.

Correct Pronunciation **Dictionary Phonetic Spelling**

1. **mode** ___ ___ ___ ___ ____________
   Meaning: ______________________________
   Sentence: ______________________________
2. **jute** ___ ___ ___ ___ ____________
   Meaning: ______________________________
   Sentence: ______________________________
3. **fame** ___ ___ ___ ___ ____________
   Meaning: ______________________________
   Sentence: ______________________________
4. **hove** ___ ___ ___ ___ ____________
   Meaning: ______________________________
   Sentence: ______________________________
5. **nape** ___ ___ ___ ___ ____________
   Meaning: ______________________________
   Sentence: ______________________________
6. **ruse** ___ ___ ___ ___ ____________
   Meaning: ______________________________
   Sentence: ______________________________
7. **cage** ___ ___ ___ ___ ____________
   Meaning: ______________________________
   Sentence: ______________________________
8. **rove** ___ ___ ___ ___ ____________
   Meaning: ______________________________
   Sentence: ______________________________
9. **mime** ___ ___ ___ ___ ____________
   Meaning: ______________________________
   Sentence: ______________________________

Name: ______________________________ Date: ____________________

Learning About Silent "e": *Reviewing Words With Short, Long, and Silent "e" Vowel Sounds*

Each of the words below has a long or short vowel sound. Many also have a silent "e" vowel. For each word write the vowel letter on the correct blank.

Word	Long Vowel Sound	Short Vowel Sound	Silent "e"
1. net	________	________	________
2. bake	________	________	________
3. base	________	________	________
4. nap	________	________	________
5. pep	________	________	________
6. pin	________	________	________
7. mate	________	________	________
8. file	________	________	________
9. fuse	________	________	________
10. mop	________	________	________
11. gum	________	________	________
12. nut	________	________	________
13. mute	________	________	________
14. tub	________	________	________
15. fast	________	________	________
16. spot	________	________	________
17. fin	________	________	________
18. fine	________	________	________
19. ton	________	________	________
20. rope	________	________	________

Name: ______________________________ Date: ____________________

Learning About the Letter "y" as a Consonant or Vowel

The letter "y" may be a consonant or a vowel. When the letter begins a word or syllable, the letter has the consonant sound.

Example: y (consonant) - **y**es be/**y**ond

The letter "y" often has a vowel sound. The vowel sound of "y" may be short "i," long "i," or long "e."

Example: y (vowel) - short "i" (g**y**m); long "i" (b**y**); long "e" (fanc**y**)

In each of the following words "y" has a consonant sound or vowel sound. Write the letter **C** (consonant) or **V** (vowel) on the blank to indicate if "y" has a consonant or vowel sound.

1. ___ yard
2. ___ merry
3. ___ my
4. ___ cry
5. ___ yam
6. ___ yes
7. ___ yesterday
8. ___ fly
9. ___ funny
10. ___ busy
11. ___ yew
12. ___ plenty
13. ___ try
14. ___ myself
15. ___ yearn

In each of the following words the letter "y" makes the short "i," long "i," or long "e" sound. If the "y" makes a short "i" sound, place the word under Column I with a breve (˘). If the "y" makes a long "i" sound, place the word under Column II with a macron (¯). If the "y" makes a long "e" sound, place the word under Column III with a macron (¯).

yap	**pony**	**year**	**dirty**	**yell**	**dye**
yarn	**cry**	**yawn**	**fry**	**yellow**	**rye**
puppy	**penny**	**you**	**yolk**	**heavy**	**snowy**
foggy	**sty**				

Column I (˘)	**Column II (¯)**	**Column III (¯)**
______________	______________	______________
______________	______________	______________
______________	______________	______________
______________	______________	______________
______________	______________	______________
______________		______________
______________		______________
______________		

Name: ______________________ Date: ______________

Learning About the Letter "y" as a Consonant or Vowel: *Reviewing the Vowel Sounds of "y"*

In words where the letter "y" follows another vowel, the letter "y" is silent.

Example: s**ay** (the long sound of "a" is heard and the letter "y" is silent.)

Pronounce each of the following words. Write the letter "S" on the blank if the letter "y" is silent.

1. ___ hay 2. ___ may 3. ___ rye 4. ___ lye
5. ___ tray 6. ___ slay 7. ___ pity

In each of the following sentences, underline the words with the letter "y." On the blank following the sentence, write **consonant**, **short i**, **long e**, **long i**, or **silent** to show the sound the letter "y" makes in the underlined word.

Sound of y

1. In the distance we could see the peak of Mount Olympus. ________
2. It was his wry humor that made us laugh. ________
3. She wore dirty jeans with a broadcloth shirt. ________
4. Later in the day it became much warmer. ________
5. The yarn he spun was too much to believe. ________
6. In parts of Southeast Asia the typhoon brings lots of rain. ________
7. In the alley behind the apartment a noise was heard. ________
8. Ireland is a land of incredible myths. ________
9. The coach said we should report to the gym. ________
10. The teacher said we must type the reports. ________
11. The spray paint covered the rust spot. ________
12. His handwriting is so sloppy. ________

Name: ______________________________ Date: ____________________

Learning About "qu": *Learning About "qu" at the Beginning of Words*

The letter "q" is often followed by the letter "u" to make the letter pair "qu." When "qu" is at the beginning of a word, then "qu" is pronounced like /kw/.

Example: **qu**ick = kwick

Each pair of words below begins with the letter pair "qu." Write the sound for the "qu" on the blank before each word. Complete the blank in each sentence using one of the pair of words.

1. ___ quack ___ quarter
   The coach said the game was won in the fourth (a) ______________.

2. ___ quiet ___ quick
   He was (a) ______________ to point out that a mistake had been made.

3. ___ queen ___ quit
   They still wonder when the (a) ______________ is going to (b) ______________.

4. ___ quiz ___ quiver
   We began to (a) ______________ when the teacher said there would be a (b) ______________ .

5. ___ quarter ___ quake
   The ground began to (a) ______________ and a (b) ______________ -hour later the volcano erupted.

6. ___ quart ___ quail
   Feed the (a) ______________ a (b) ______________ of grain.

Name: ______________________________ Date: ____________________

Learning About "qu": *Learning About "qu" at the End of Words*

In many words, the letter pair "qu" does not appear at the beginning of a word. The "qu" pair may occur in the middle or at the end of a word. When "qu" is in the middle or at the end of a word, the sound of "qu" is usually /k/.

Example: bou**qu**et = bō kā′

The combination "que" comes at the end of many words. When "que" comes at the end of a word, this letter combination is usually pronounced as /k/.

In Column II on the right is the dictionary spelling for each word in Column I. Match the dictionary spelling in Collumn II with the correct word in Column I.

		Column I		Column II
______	1.	antique	a.	ō pāk′
______	2.	opaque	b.	tĕk nēk′
______	3.	technique	c.	ăn tēk′
______	4.	unique	d.	grō tĕsk′
______	5.	grotesque	e.	yo͞o nēk′
______	6.	bouquet	f.	bo͞o tēk′
______	7.	banquet	g.	bō kā′
______	8.	boutique	h.	klēk
______	9.	clique	i.	băng′ kwət
______	10.	banquette	j.	băng kĕt′

Name: ______________________________ Date: ________________

Learning About "qu": *Using Words With "qu"*

Complete each of the blanks using one of the following words.

banquet	**bouquet**	**antique**	**unique**	**clique**
opaque	**technique**	**grotesque**	**boutique**	**banquette**

1. When we go to the city, my sister insists on finding a ________________ to shop at.
2. She bought the chair in an ________________ store.
3. The light could not be seen through the ________________ window.
4. Our art teacher taught us a very ________________ way to paint.
5. The statue was so ugly, many said it was ________________.
6. We sat on a ________________ while waiting to get a table in the restaurant.
7. We arrived at the ________________ just as the food and drinks were served.
8. He gave her a beautiful ________________ of roses.
9. They do not want others in their friendship group; they are a ________________.
10. The artist used a special ________________ to paint the landscape.

Name: ______________________ Date: ______________

Learning About "c," "g," and "s": *The Consonant "c"*

When the consonant "c" is followed by the letters "a," "o," or "u," the "c" is pronounced as /k/.

Example: The "c" in cat is pronounced as /k/. When "c" is sounded as /k/, it is called the **hard** sound of "c."

When the consonant "c" is followed by the letters "i," "e," or "y," the "c" is pronounced as /s/.

Example: The "c" in city is pronounced as /s/. When "c" is sounded as /s/, it is called the **soft** sound of "c."

Pronounce each of the following words. If the "c" is the hard sound, place /k/ on the blank before the word. If the letter "c" is the soft sound, place /s/ on the blank before the word. Complete the blanks under each heading.

		vowels sounded	long/short	silent	sound of y
1.	___ cape	______	______	______	
2.	___ cane	______	______	______	
3.	___ cite	______	______	______	
4.	___ cent	______	______	______	
5.	___ cage	______	______	______	
6.	___ came	______	______	______	
7.	___ city	______	______	______	______
8.	___ cell	______	______	______	
9.	___ copy	______	______	______	______
10.	___ cyst	______	______	______	______
11.	___ center	______	______	______	
12.	___ cement	______	______	______	
13.	___ crime	______	______	______	
14.	___ cone	______	______	______	
15.	___ cube	______	______	______	

16. In all the words having the hard "c" sound, the "c" is followed by the vowels ___, ___, or ___.
17. In all the words having the soft "c" sound, the "c" is followed by the letters ___, ___, or ___.

Name: ______________________________ Date: ____________________

Learning About "c," "g," and "s": *The Consonant "g"*

The consonant "g" has a **hard sound** and a **soft sound**. When the consonant "g" is followed by the letters "a," "o," or "u," the "g" is hard. The sound of "g" is hard in the word "**go**." When the consonant "g" is followed by the letters "i," "e," or "y," the "g" is soft. The sound of "g" is soft in the word "**gym**."

Each of the words below begins with the consonant "g." Complete the blank in each sentence using one of the words in bold. Write the letter "h" or "s" in the parentheses to indicate if the consonant "g" has a hard or soft sound. Use the dictionary to determine the meaning of words.

gaunt	**gem**	**gyrate**	**geometry**	**gallery**
garland	**ginger**	**generous**	**galaxy**	**gutter**

1. We are going to study ( ) ______________ this evening.
2. She does many things to help others; she is a ( ) ______________ person.
3. The ( ) ______________ plant is important in medicine and cooking.
4. He bought her a ( ) ______________ for her birthday.
5. The runners on the track team are all ( ) ______________ fellows.
6. It was difficult to determine directions after the compass began to ( ) ______________ wildly.
7. When I arrived in Hawaii, a ( ) ______________ of flowers was placed around my neck.
8. If you look into the night, the Milky Way ( ) ______________ can be seen.
9. We went to the ( ) ______________ to see the display of art work.
10. The carpenter placed a ( ) ______________ on the house to drain the water from the roof.

Use each of the following words in a sentence. On the blank indicate if the letter "g" has a hard or soft sound.

1. **gale** _____ hard _____ soft
   Sentence: ______________________________
2. **general** _____ hard _____ soft
   Sentence: ______________________________
3. **garment** _____ hard _____ soft
   Sentence: ______________________________

Name: ______________________________ Date: ____________________

Learning About "c," "g," and "s": *The Consonant "s"*

The consonant letter "s" has a hard sound and a soft sound. The **soft sound** is pronounced with an /s/ sound. The **hard sound** is pronounced with a /z/ sound. Pronounce each of the words in the exercise below. Place an /s/ or /z/ on the blank before each word to indicate if the sound is /s/ or /z/.

1. ___ sack	2. ___ babies	3. ___ boys	4. ___ soup
5. ___ second	6. ___ frogs	7. ___ chairs	8. ___ please
9. ___ settle	10. ___ single	11. ___ cookies	12. ___ rose
13. ___ satin	14. ___ send		

15. Each of the following words has the consonant letter "s." If the "s" makes an /s/ sound, place the word in Column I. Place those words with "s" making a /z/ sound in Column II.

sack	**babies**	**boys**	**soup**	**second**	**frogs**	**satin**
chairs	**please**	**settle**	**single**	**cookies**	**rose**	**send**

Column I /s/		**Column II /z/**	
__________	__________	__________	__________
__________	__________	__________	__________
__________	__________	__________	__________
__________		__________	

Circle the correct answer.

16. When the letter "s" begins a word, the sound is (a) /s/ (b) /z/.
17. When the letter "s" is at the end of a word, the sound is (a) /s/ (b) /z/.

Each of the sentences below has a word in bold. Indicate if the sound of "s" is /s/ or /z/ in the bold word by placing a check mark on the appropriate line.

18. Our **families** plan to spend Thanksgiving together. ____ /s/ ____ /z/
19. It is very important to **please** one's parents. ____ /s/ ____ /z/
20. They will place the cans of fruit on the **shelves**. ____ /s/ ____ /z/
21. The party was a great **surprise** to both of them. ____ /s/ ____ /z/
22. They wanted us to tell them two funny **stories**. ____ /s/ ____ /z/
23. The two nations have been **enemies** for many years. ____ /s/ ____ /z/

Name: ______________________________ Date: ____________________

Learning About "c," "g," and "s": *Understanding Phonetic Spelling*

When using the dictionary, the phonetic spelling of a word helps you pronounce the word. Column I on the left lists the dictionary phonetic spelling of common words that contain the sounds of "c," "g," and "s." Write the correct spelling of the word on the blank in Column II.

	Column I	Column II	Definition
1.	kăn′ dē	____________	good to eat
2.	gĕst	____________	recipient of hospitality
3.	kăn′ səl	____________	draw lines across
4.	sīt	____________	mention specifically
5.	glār	____________	dazzling light
6.	jī′ rō	____________	a ring or circle
7.	sĭv′ əl	____________	refers to the state and its laws
8.	jĕl′ ə tĭn	____________	jellylike
9.	glĭmps	____________	quick look or glance
10.	sĭnch	____________	something sure to be accomplished
11.	sī′ klōn	____________	a storm of great destruction
12.	kro͞o sād′	____________	to support a cause
13.	găj′ ĭt	____________	small mechanical device
14.	gā′ lē	____________	merrily
15.	kăn′ dĭd	____________	outspoken, frank
16.	jĭp	____________	cheat or swindle
17.	kōm	____________	used to groom hair
18.	gōst	____________	a spirit
19.	sĭm′ bəl	____________	musical instrument
20.	glīd	____________	move with smooth easy motion

Name: ______________________ Date: ______________

Learning About "c," "g," and "s": *Reviewing the Sounds of "c," "g," and "s"*

Pronounce each of the following words. Place a check mark on the blank to show the sound the consonant in bold makes. Write a sentence using the word.

1. **c**ontrol ____ /k/ ____ /s/

   Sentence: ______________________

2. **g**alore ____ hard ____ soft

   Sentence: ______________________

3. **c**ement ____ /k/ ____ /s/

   Sentence: ______________________

4. **c**edar ____ /k/ ____ /s/

   Sentence: ______________________

5. **g**erm ____ hard ____ soft

   Sentence: ______________________

6. **s**ample ____ /s/ ____ /z/

   Sentence: ______________________

7. wive**s** ____ /s/ ____ /z/

   Sentence: ______________________

8. **g**ypsy ____ hard ____ soft

   Sentence: ______________________

9. loo**s**e ____ /s/ ____ /z/

   Sentence: ______________________

10. **c**apital ____ /k/ ____ /s/

    Sentence: ______________________

Name: ____________________ Date: ____________

Learning About "c," "g," and "s": *More Reviewing "c," "g," and "s"*

Complete the blanks in each of the following sentences using the letters "c," "g," or "s." Then place a check mark on the correct blank to show which sound of the letter "c," "g," or "s" is in the blank. The first one is completed for you.

1. The tail of the comet made a bright light in the night sky.

   (a) _✓_ k ____ s (b) _✓_ s ____ z

2. Sam will be the team ___aptain for the next ___ame.

   (a) _✓_ k ____ s (b) ____ soft _✓_ hard

3. The ___ale blew just as we be___an to ___ail.

   (a) ____ soft ____ hard (b) ____ soft ____ hard (c) ____ s ____ z

4. In many European countries, ___yp___ie___ travel from place to place.

   (a) ____ soft ____ hard (b) ____ s ____ z (c) ____ s ____ z

5. The ___uests were all enjoying the ___arden party when the ___torm began.

   (a) ____ soft ____ hard (b) ____ soft ____ hard (c) ____ s ____ z

6. For breakfa___t we had ___ereal and toa___t.

   (a) ____ s ____ z (b) ____ k ____ s (c) ____ s ____ z

7. We ate ___elery because it has few ___alorie___.

   (a) ____ k ____ s (b) ____ k ____ s (c) ____ s ____ z

8. That is ___enuine ___edar that can be used for the ___able on the hou___e.

   (a) ____ soft ____hard (b) ____ k ____ s (c) ____ soft ____ hard

   (d) ____ s ____ z

9. When we finish the ___eometry le___son, we ___an play ___olf.

   (a) ____ soft ____ hard (b) ____ z ____ s (c) ____ k ____ s

   (d) ____ soft ____ hard

10. They had a ___allon of ___ider and a ___arrot.

    (a) ____ soft ____ hard (b) ____ k ____ s (c) ____ k ____ s

Name: ______________________ Date: ______________

Learning About "x"

The consonant "x" may have the sound /ks/, /gz/, or /z/.

Examples: **/ks/**: so**x**
/gz/: e**x**ile
/z/: **x**ylophone

Determine the sound of "x" in each of the following words. Place **ks**, **gz**, or **z** on the blank next to the word to show the sound of "x" in the word. Use each word in a sentence. Use a dictionary if you are unsure of the meaning or pronunciation of a word.

1. **fix** ________
   Sentence: ______________________________
2. **xylem** ________
   Sentence: ______________________________
3. **exit** ________
   Sentence: ______________________________
4. **axis** ________
   Sentence: ______________________________
5. **exist** ________
   Sentence: ______________________________
6. **index** ________
   Sentence: ______________________________
7. **xenon** ________
   Sentence: ______________________________
8. **examine** ________
   Sentence: ______________________________
9. **xebec** ________
   Sentence: ______________________________
10. **vertex** ________
    Sentence: ______________________________

Name: ______________________________ Date: ____________________

Learning About Consonant Blends: *Making Words Using Beginning Consonant Blends*

Consonant blends are two- or three-letter consonants that are blended together when sounded in a word.

Examples: blind = **bl**ind trust = **tr**ust

Use the following blends and make new words that match the meanings. Then write the word on the blank using the macron (¯) to show the long vowel sound and a slash (/) to show the silent "e" for each word. Write the new word in a sentence that matches the meaning.

fl bl gr gl br fr sl cl dr pl pr

1. ___ ___ide ______________ meaning: slip over a smooth surface
Sentence: ____
2. ___ ___ave ______________ meaning: burial site
Sentence: ____
3. ___ ___aze ______________ meaning: brush lightly in passing
Sentence: ____
4. ___ ___ute ______________ meaning: musical instrument
Sentence: ____
5. ___ ___ose ______________ meaning: finish or conclude
Sentence: ____
6. ___ ___ue ______________ meaning: a hint
Sentence: ____
7. ___ ___ape ______________ meaning: fruit used to make jelly
Sentence: ____
8. ___ ___are ______________ meaning: blazing light used as a signal
Sentence: ____
9. ___ ___ame ______________ meaning: to hold responsible for error
Sentence: ____
10. ___ ___ade ______________ meaning: clear space in a forest
Sentence: ____
11. ___ ___ipe ______________ meaning: to complain
Sentence: ____
12. ___ ___obe ______________ meaning: to search or explore
Sentence: ____

Name: ______________________________ Date: ________________

Learning About Consonant Blends: *More Work With Blends*

Replace the blends in the words in the column under **Word** with one of the blends below to make a new word. Choose a blend to make a new word that rhymes. Show the correct markings for long vowel sounds and silent letters. Use the new word in a sentence.

dr bl sm pr tr sl gr spl gl

Word	New Word	New Word With Markings for Vowel Sound and Silent Letters
1. **slate**	__ __ate	__________
Sentence: __________		
2. **slope**	__ __ope	__________
Sentence: __________		
3. **trade**	__ __ade	__________
Sentence: __________		
4. **crime**	__ __ime	__________
Sentence: __________		
5. **slice**	__ __ __ice	__________
Sentence: __________		
6. **frame**	__ __ame	__________
Sentence: __________		
7. **clove**	__ __ove	__________
Sentence: __________		
8. **craze**	__ __aze	__________
Sentence: __________		
9. **bloke**	__ __oke	__________
Sentence: __________		
10. **flake**	__ __ake	__________
Sentence: __________		

   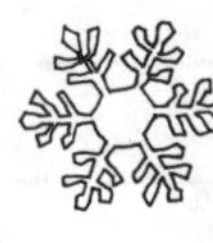

Name: ______________________ Date: ______________

Learning About Consonant Blends: *More Work With Blends*

For each of the following words, underline the blend. Write the vowel that makes the long sound on the blank in Column I. Write the silent letter on the blank in Column II. Show the dictionary pronunciation in Column III.

Word	Column I	Column II	Column III
1. scribe	______	______	____________
2. slime	______	______	____________
3. prime	______	______	____________
4. frame	______	______	____________
5. fluke	______	______	____________
6. crone	______	______	____________
7. grope	______	______	____________
8. blade	______	______	____________
9. brine	______	______	____________
10. clove	______	______	____________

Use each of the words from the list above in sentences.

1. ____
2. ____
3. ____
4. ____
5. ____
6. ____
7. ____
8. ____
9. ____
10. ____

Name: ______________________________ Date: ____________________

Learning About Consonant Blends: *Making and Using Words With Ending Consonant Blends*

In many words, the two letters at the end of the word are **consonant blends**. These are consonant pairs with the sound of both consonants sounded.

Each of the words in the column at the right ends with one of the consonant blends: **ft**, **lk**, **lb**, **nk**, **nt**, **ld**, or **nd**. Choose one of the words on the right to complete the blank found in each sentence. On the blank after the sentence, write the letters that make the ending blend found in the word used to complete the sentence.

	Ending Blend	
1. After the boat sank, the crew was __________ at sea.	_____	**blank**
2. He took the shirt back to the store for a __________.	_____	**bulb**
3. The riders were told to __________ the horses.	_____	**bulk**
4. He was being punished for the __________.	_____	**adrift**
5. The pirates were often very __________.	_____	**prank**
6. The tulip __________ should be planted in the fall.	_____	**refund**
7. They stood with a __________ look on their faces.	_____	**mount**
8. The __________ of the goods arrived yesterday.	_____	**bold**

The two-letter consonant blends "**ng**," "**nk**," "**pt**," "**st**," and "**sp**" are often found at the end of words. Match the definition with the correct word. Write the ending consonant blend for each word on the blank provided.

	Word	Ending Consonant Blend	Definition
_____	1. prong	________	a. edge, like a cliff
_____	2. adapt	________	b. unpleasantly damp
_____	3. brink	________	c. brittle or crumbly
_____	4. wrest	________	d. alter to make suitable
_____	5. crisp	________	e. skillful or expert
_____	6. slang	________	f. a sharp point
_____	7. dank	________	g. not apt or suited
_____	8. inept	________	h. seize by violent twisting
_____	9. adept	________	i. grain to be ground
_____	10. grist	________	j. coarse language

Name: ______________________________ Date: ____________________

Learning About Consonant Blends: *Reviewing Consonant Blends*

The following words have beginning and/or ending blends. Write the word on the blank. Circle the blend(s). Then write the blend(s) on the blanks following the word. Finally, write a sentence using each of the following words.

bland bloke braid brute graft oft clone click stalk gland

	Word	Beginning Blend	Vowel Sound long/short/silent	Ending Blend
1.	________	____	________	____

Sentence: ______________________________

	Word	Beginning Blend	Vowel Sound long/short/silent	Ending Blend
2.	________	____	________	____

Sentence: ______________________________

3. ________ ____ ________ ____

Sentence: ______________________________

4. ________ ____ ________ ____

Sentence: ______________________________

5. ________ ____ ________ ____

Sentence: ______________________________

6. ________ ____ ________ ____

Sentence: ______________________________

7. ________ ____ ________ ____

Sentence: ______________________________

8. ________ ____ ________ ____

Sentence: ______________________________

9. ________ ____ ________ ____

Sentence: ______________________________

10. ________ ____ ________ ____

Sentence: ______________________________

Name: __________________________ Date: __________________

Learning to Read Words With Vowel Pairs: *Learning About the "ai" Vowel Pair*

In each of the following sentences, you will find a word with the letters "ai." When these two letters are together, they make the long sound of the letter "a." Complete the blank in each sentence using one of the words below.

frail rain maize braise train taint maims paint sail raise

1. Farmers __________ grains like corn, oats, and beans.
2. The ship will __________ on time, so we must not be late.
3. The clouds became dark, the wind blew, and the __________ fell.
4. He had been sick and looked __________.
5. Artists must be in the right mood to __________.
6. When we arrived at the station, the __________ had left.
7. You must __________ the meat to make a stew.
8. The lie he told left a __________ on his reputation.
9. Native Americans raised crops including __________.
10. War often __________ the soldiers who serve.

Place each of the following words under the column that describes the vowel sounds and blends in the word. A word may be placed under more than one column.

saint gift paint blast faint globe cope
sprint flail trail glob gait lot rang

Long Vowel Sound	Short Vowel Sound	Silent Vowel	Beginning Blend	Ending Blend

Name: ______________________ Date: ______________

Learning to Read Words With Vowel Pairs: *Learning About the "ai" Vowel Pair*

Place one of the following consonants or blends on the blank to make a word with the long "a" sound. Next, write the complete word on the blank under Column I. Then, write the vowel pair that makes the long "a" sound on the blank under Column II. Finally, write a sentence using each word.

pr q str tr w r cl pl f p

	Column I	**Column II**
1. ___aid	______________	_____
Sentence: ______________________		
2. ___ail	______________	_____
Sentence: ______________________		
3. ___ain	______________	_____
Sentence: ______________________		
4. ___ait	______________	_____
Sentence: ______________________		
5. ___ ___aise	______________	_____
Sentence: ______________________		
6. ___ ___aim	______________	_____
Sentence: ______________________		
7. ___ ___ain	______________	_____
Sentence: ______________________		
8. ___uaint	______________	_____
Sentence: ______________________		
9. ___ ___ ___ait	______________	_____
Sentence: ______________________		
10. ___aith	______________	_____
Sentence: ______________________		

Name: ______________________ Date: ______________

Learning to Read Words With Vowel Pairs: *Learning About the "ay" Vowel Pair*

When the "ay" vowel pair is found together, it makes the long sound of the letter "a." In each sentence below is a word in bold that has the dictionary spelling for an "ay" word. On the blank at the end of each sentence, write the correct spelling for the "ay" word. Below is a list of meanings for the words in bold. Select the meaning for each word in bold and write the meaning on the blank below each sentence.

Definitions: a race among teams of runners • strip the skin from • low, horse-drawn cart for heavy loads • a wandering animal or person • a bird • harsh cry of a mule or donkey • fine mist of water • flat, shallow box for holding something • a battle or skirmish • no, a refusal

1. The **brā** of the mule could be heard for miles. bray
   Meaning: ______________________
2. He walked through the cafeteria with a **trā** of food. tray
   Meaning: ______________________
3. After the **frā** was over, the home team had won. fray
   Meaning: ______________________
4. The team of horses pulled the **drā** loaded with wood. dray
   Meaning: ______________________
5. He answered **nā** to the questions. nay
   Meaning: ______________________
6. They will **flā** the skin from the fish they caught. flay
   Meaning: ______________________
7. The bird on the limb was a **bluejā**. bluejay
   Meaning: ______________________
8. She is a member of the school **rēlā** team. relay
   Meaning: ______________________
9. A **strā** cat was sitting on the fence. stray
   Meaning: ______________________
10. She will **sprā** the car with water. spray
    Meaning: ______________________

Name: ______________________________ Date: ____________________

Learning to Read Words With Vowel Pairs: *Learning About the "ay" Vowel Pair*

Place one of the following sets of letters on each blank to make a word. Next, write the complete word on the blanks under Column I. Then, write the letter that indicates the sound of "ay" on the blank under Column II, using the macron to show the sound of the letter under Column II. Finally, write a sentence using the word.

sl de spr cr pr br gr fl spl cl

	Column I	Column II
1. __ __ay	__________	___
Sentence: ____________________		
2. __ __cay	__________	___
Sentence: ____________________		
3. __ __ __ay	__________	___
Sentence: ____________________		
4. __ __ayon	__________	___
Sentence: ____________________		
5. __ __ay	__________	___
Sentence: ____________________		
6. __ __ay	__________	___
Sentence: ____________________		
7. __ __ay	__________	___
Sentence: ____________________		
8. __ __ay	__________	___
Sentence: ____________________		
9. __ __ __ay	__________	___
Sentence: ____________________		
10. __ __ay	__________	___
Sentence: ____________________		

Name: ______________________ Date: ______________

Learning to Read Words With Vowel Pairs: *Reviewing the Vowel Pairs "ai" and "ay"*

Each of the sentences below contains two words in bold with a dictionary spelling. The words in bold are "ai" and "ay" words. Write the correct spelling for each "ai" word on the blank under Column I. Write the correct spelling for each "ay" word on the blank under Column II.

	Column I	Column II
1. We saw a **frāl grā**-headed man.	______	______
2. **Strāt** and **bā** are geography terms.	______	______
3. The **strā** horse was eating **māze**.	______	______
4. Use a **grā crāon** for your art work.	______	______
5. The **mān** rule was to **plā** fair.	______	______
6. On the **chāse** was a **trā** of food.	______	______
7. Did you **pā** for the **bāt**?	______	______
8. On the **trān** a man began to **prā**.	______	______
9. Did he **sprā pānt** on the house?	______	______
10. After the **rē′ lā** race, she felt **fānt**.	______	______

Use ten of the words from above in sentences of your own below.

1. ______________________________
2. ______________________________
3. ______________________________
4. ______________________________
5. ______________________________
6. ______________________________
7. ______________________________
8. ______________________________
9. ______________________________
10. ______________________________

Name: ______________________ Date: ______________

Learning to Read Words With Vowel Pairs: *Unscrambling Letters to Make "ai" or "ay" Words*

Each of the set of scrambled letters can be used to make a word with the vowel pairs "ai" or "ay." Unscramble each set of letters to make a word with the long "a" sound. Write the word made from the scrambled letters on the blank. Indicate if the vowel pair is "ai" or "ay." Circle long "a" or short "a" to show the vowel sound. Finally, write a sentence using the unscrambled word.

	Word	ai/ay Vowel Pair	Vowel Sound of ai or ay
1. aplin	________	____	long "a"/short "a"
Sentence:			
2. ryaf	________	____	long "a"/short "a"
Sentence:			
3. yan	________	____	long "a"/short "a"
Sentence:			
4. rispea	________	____	long "a"/short "a"
Sentence:			
5. gnai	________	____	long "a"/short "a"
Sentence:			
6. taig	________	____	long "a"/short "a"
Sentence:			
7. rsyat	________	____	long "a"/short "a"
Sentence:			
8. ntair	________	____	long "a"/short "a"
Sentence:			
9. zamie	________	____	long "a"/short "a"
Sentence:			
10. ttair	________	____	long "a"/short "a"
Sentence:			
11. lfail	________	____	long "a"/short "a"
Sentence:			

Name: ______________________________ Date: ___________________

Learning to Read Words With Vowel Pairs: *Learning About the "ea" Vowel Pair*

Many words have the vowel pair "ea." The vowel pair "ea" usually makes the long "e" vowel sound.

Example: In the word "bean" the "ea" is sounded as "e."

In each of the following sentences, you will find a word in bold that is the dictionary spelling of an "ea" word. Write the "ea" word the dictionary spelling stands for in Column II. Then circle "long" or "short" for the vowel sound and write the vowel letter that represents the sound of "ea" on the blank in Column III.

Column I	Column II	Column III
1. It is a **blēk** winter day.	__________	long/short ___
2. The **hēp** of rocks must be moved.	__________	long/short ___
3. His **skrēm** scared all of us.	__________	long/short ___
4. It was hot, so we went to the **bēch**.	__________	long/short ___
5. Sheep **blēt** when they are hungry.	__________	long/short ___
6. You must **knēd** the dough before baking.	__________	long/short ___
7. **Ēch** one of you must be on time.	__________	long/short ___
8. The **brēch** in the levee caused a flood.	__________	long/short ___
9. Go to the office and get a **rēm** of paper.	__________	long/short ___
10. High above us an **ē′ gəl** soared.	__________	long/short ___

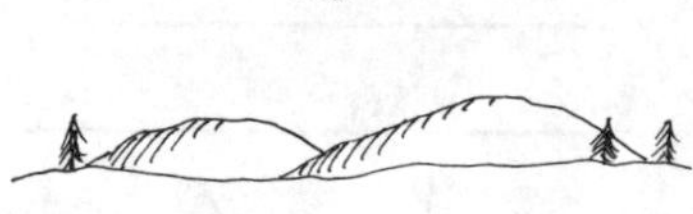

Name: ______________________________ Date: ____________________

Learning to Read Words With Vowel Pairs: *Using Blends to Make "ea" Words With the Long Sound*

Place one of the following consonant blends on the blank to make a word with a long "e" sound. Write the word on the blanks under Column I. Write the letters that make the long "e" sound on the blanks under Column II. Write a sentence using the word.

dr tr pr st gl br bl sl cl scr

	Column I	**Column II**
1. ___ ___eat	____________	_____
Sentence: ______________________________		
2. ___ ___ean	____________	_____
Sentence: ______________________________		
3. ___ ___each	____________	_____
Sentence: ______________________________		
4. ___ ___eal	____________	_____
Sentence: ______________________________		
5. ___ ___ ___eam	____________	_____
Sentence: ______________________________		
6. ___ ___eat	____________	_____
Sentence: ______________________________		
7. ___ ___eat	____________	_____
Sentence: ______________________________		
8. ___ ___eam	____________	_____
Sentence: ______________________________		
9. ___ ___ean	____________	_____
Sentence: ______________________________		
10. ___ ___each	____________	_____
Sentence: ______________________________		
11. ___ ___eam	____________	_____
Sentence: ______________________________		
12. ___ ___eam	____________	_____
Sentence: ______________________________		

Name: ______________________________ Date: ____________________

Learning to Read Words With Vowel Pairs: *Other "ea" Sounds*

You have learned that when a word has the "ea" vowel pair, it usually makes the long "e" sound. However, there are many words with "ea" that are pronounced with the short "e" sound. Generally, you need to read the word in a sentence to know how to pronounce it. If the word does not make sense pronounced with a long "e" sound, try pronouncing it with a short "e" sound.

Example: "ea" word with long "e" sound = scream
I heard him scream.

Example: "ea" word with short "e" sound = tread
The tread on the tire is worn smooth.

In each of the following sentences, a word is in bold. The "ea" letter pair makes the short "e" sound in some words and the long "e" sound in others. Read the sentence and check the blank beside short "e" or long "e" to show the sound of "ea" in the word in bold.

1. Do you **dread** going to the dentist? ____ short e ____ long e
2. They said our **treat** would be pizza. ____ short e ____ long e
3. He left the meeting with a **heavy** heart. ____ short e ____ long e
4. We plan to go to the **beach** on Saturday. ____ short e ____ long e
5. The **creak** of the door scared everyone. ____ short e ____ long e
6. The **flea** jumped from the dog to the boy. ____ short e ____ long e
7. He **read** the chapter before the test. ____ short e ____ long e
8. The **steam** ship left the port on time. ____ short e ____ long e
9. At the store, they bought a **peach** and an apple. ____ short e ____ long e
10. You will need a needle and **thread**. ____ short e ____ long e

Name: ______________________________ Date: ____________________

Learning to Read Words With Vowel Pairs: *Reviewing What Has Been Learned*

Underline the letters that make the long or short vowel sound in each word. Write the letters that make the long or short vowel sound on the blank under Column I. Write the vowel letter and macron (¯) or breve (˘) symbol that indicates the sound of the two underlined letters on the blank under Column II. Under Column III circle "long" or "short" to indicate the sound of the vowel pair.

Word	Column I	Column II	Column III
1. snail	___ ___	___	long/short
2. bleak	___ ___	___	long/short
3. exclaim	___ ___	___	long/short
4. claim	___ ___	___	long/short
5. sway	___ ___	___	long/short
6. stray	___ ___	___	long/short
7. again	___ ___	___	long/short
8. frail	___ ___	___	long/short
9. spread	___ ___	___	long/short
10. delay	___ ___	___	long/short
11. thread	___ ___	___	long/short
12. cease	___ ___	___	long/short
13. away	___ ___	___	long/short
14. leach	___ ___	___	long/short
15. bread	___ ___	___	long/short

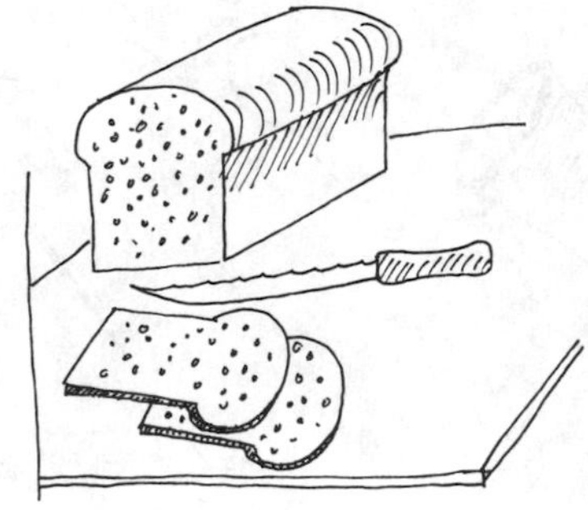

Name: ______________________________ Date: ________________

Learning to Read Words With Vowel Pairs: *More Vowel Pair Review*

Circle "long" or "short" and fill in the blank with the correct vowel for each word.

1. We will reach the beach by rail, and then we will sail.
   (a) The "ea" in reach is sounded as long/short ____.
   (b) The "ea" in beach is sounded as long/short ____.
   (c) The "ai" in sail is sounded as long/short ____.
2. I read that the delay of the game was because of rain.
   (a) The "ea" in read is sounded as long/short ____.
   (b) The "ay" in delay is sounded as long/short ____.
   (c) The "ai" in rain is sounded as long/short ____.
3. She leads the bay mule to the barn to eat grain.
   (a) The "ea" in leads is sounded as long/short ____.
   (b) The "ay" in bay is sounded as long/short ____.
   (c) The "ea" in eat is sounded as long/short ____.
   (d) The "ai" in grain is sounded as long/short ____.

4. The tea was cheap so I paid for the treat.
   (a) The "ea" in tea is sounded as long/short ____.
   (b) The "ea" in cheap is sounded as long/short ____.
   (c) The "ai" in paid is sounded as long/short ____.
   (d) The "ea" in treat is sounded as long/short ____.
5. The stream meanders in a braidlike manner.
   (a) The "ea" in stream is sounded as long/short ____.
   (b) The "ai" in braid is sounded as long/short ____.
6. A saint will pray and read each day.
   (a) The "ai" in saint is sounded as long/short ____.
   (b) The "ay" in pray is sounded as long/short ____.
   (c) The "ea" in read is sounded as long/short ____.
   (d) The "ea" in each is sounded as long/short ____.
   (e) The "ay" in day is sounded as long/short ____.
7. Put the peaches on the tray next to the bread.
   (a) The "ea" in peaches is sounded as long/short ____.
   (b) The "ay" in tray is sounded as long/short ____.
   (c) The "ea" in bread is sounded as long/short ____.

Name: ______________________ Date: ______________

Learning to Read Words With Vowel Pairs: *Learning About the "ee" Vowel Pair*

In the exercise below, you will find words with the letter pair "ee." When these two letters are together, they make the long sound of the letter "e." The list in bold below contains the dictionary phonetic spelling for words with the "ee" pair. Write the dictionary phonetic spelling on the blank next to the correct spelling of the word. Identify the meaning of each word from the list at the bottom of the page and write it on the blank below each word.

prēn brēch pēv rēk hēd dēm wēp stēpl lēch twēd

Correct Spelling **Dictionary Spelling**

1. **deem** ______________
   Meaning: ______________________________
2. **breech** ______________
   Meaning: ______________________________
3. **tweed** ______________
   Meaning: ______________________________
4. **peeve** ______________
   Meaning: ______________________________
5. **weep** ______________
   Meaning: ______________________________
6. **heed** ______________
   Meaning: ______________________________
7. **steeple** ______________
   Meaning: ______________________________
8. **preen** ______________
   Meaning: ______________________________
9. **leech** ______________
   Meaning: ______________________________
10. **reek** ______________
    Meaning: ______________________________

Definitions: part of a gun behind the barrel • to pay careful attention or observe carefully • to trim or dress the feathers with the beak • a coarse, wool cloth • lofty tower or structure attached to a church • blood-sucking aquatic worm • to form or have an opinion • to cry or mourn • strong or unpleasant smell • to be cross or annoyed

Name: ______________________________ Date: ________________

Learning to Read Words With Vowel Pairs: *Using Consonant Blends to Make "ee" Words*

Place one of the following consonant blends on the blanks to make a word. Write the word on the blank under Column I. Then write the letters that make the long "e" sound on the blanks under Column II. Finally, write a sentence using the word.

spl wh gr fr scr sl cr fl br

	Column I	Column II
1. __ __eed	____________	__ __
2. __ __eet	____________	__ __
3. __ __ __eech	____________	__ __
4. __ __eed	____________	__ __
5. __ __eece	____________	__ __
6. __ __ __een	____________	__ __
7. __ __eeze	____________	__ __
8. __ __een	____________	__ __
9. __ __eeze	____________	__ __
10. __ __ __een	____________	__ __

1. __ __eed ____________ __ __

Sentence: ______________________________

2. __ __eet ____________ __ __

Sentence: ______________________________

3. __ __ __eech ____________ __ __

Sentence: ______________________________

4. __ __eed ____________ __ __

Sentence: ______________________________

5. __ __eece ____________ __ __

Sentence: ______________________________

6. __ __ __een ____________ __ __

Sentence: ______________________________

7. __ __eeze ____________ __ __

Sentence: ______________________________

8. __ __een ____________ __ __

Sentence: ______________________________

9. __ __eeze ____________ __ __

Sentence: ______________________________

10. __ __ __een ____________ __ __

Sentence: ______________________________

Name: ______________________________ Date: ____________________

Learning to Read Words With Vowel Pairs: *Reviewing Words With the Vowel Pairs "ai," "ay," "ea," or "ee"*

Circle the words in each sentence with the vowel pair "ai," "ay," "ea," or "ee."

1. The maize and hay are feed for the beast.
2. The faint queen could not read the speech.
3. The steeple of the church could be seen from the street.
4. To make bread, the maid must knead the dough and place it in a tray.
5. Today, many people have great pain and weep when their team is in the fray.
6. It was a great gray beast from the deep.
7. He dreamed the ship would sail through the strait and out to sea.
8. I read that a meal for a small fee is a real deal.
9. Today the lean queen ate a meal of meat and maize.
10. He would sneeze and wheeze when the hay was baled.
11. The snail in the pail became a meal.
12. Will Ray deem it necessary to display his train set at the show?
13. The jail reeked of sweat and tears.
14. I would weep if a leech touched my breeches.
15. Spray the paint from the pail on the quaint house by the beach.

Name: ______________________________ Date: ____________________

Learning to Read Words With Vowel Pairs: *Learning About the "oa" Vowel Pair*

The letter pair "oa" makes the long "o" sound. Place the following consonants on the blanks to make a word. Write the word on the blank under Column I. Write the letters that make the long "o" sound on the blank under Column II. Write a sentence using the word.

k c thr gl b fl br r

	Column I	**Column II**
1. ___ ___oat	____________	____
Sentence: ________________________		
2. ___ ___oat	____________	____
Sentence: ________________________		
3. ___ oat	____________	____
Sentence: ________________________		
4. ___ ___oast	____________	____
Sentence: ________________________		
5. ___ ___oach	____________	____
Sentence: ________________________		
6. ___oach	____________	____
Sentence: ________________________		
7. oa___	____________	____
Sentence: ________________________		
8. ___ ___ ___oat	____________	____
Sentence: ________________________		
9. ___oat	____________	____
Sentence: ________________________		
10. ___oast	____________	____
Sentence: ________________________		

Name: ______________________________ Date: ____________________

Learning to Read Words With Vowel Pairs: *Unscrambling Letters to Make Words With the "oa" Vowel Pair*

Unscramble the letters below to match the definition. Write the unscrambled word on the blank. Circle "long" or "short" and complete the blank to show the sound of the vowel.

		Scrambled Word	Unscrambled Word	Vowel Sound
1.	to brag	asbot	____________	long/short ___
2.	to bake as in an oven	oarst	____________	long/short ___
3.	a kind of tree	ako	____________	long/short ___
4.	low sound made when in pain	naom	____________	long/short ___
5.	to utter a sound like a frog	ckora	____________	long/short ___
6.	land area near the ocean	tcaos	____________	long/short ___
7.	passage from mouth to lungs	rhtota	____________	long/short ___
8.	a kind of soil	mloa	____________	long/short ___
9.	to take game or fish illegally	cohpa	____________	long/short ___
10.	to persuade gently	xaco	____________	long/short ___

Use each of the words above in a sentence.

1. ____
2. ____
3. ____
4. ____
5. ____
6. ____
7. ____
8. ____
9. ____
10. ____

Name: ______________________________ Date: ________________

Learning to Read Words With Vowel Pairs: *Reviewing What Has Been Learned*

Read each of the following sentences. Read the directions by each sentence and write the answer on the blank below each sentence.

1. The man with the long mane began to boast.
   (Write the words that have short "a," long "a," and long "o" sounds.)

   ____

2. Each day we went to the coast to see the boats sail.
   (Write the words with long "e," long "a," and long "o" sounds.)

   ____

3. The green yeast would make bread to toast.
   (Write the words with long "e," long "a," short "e," and long "o" sounds.)

   ____

4. The moan of the coach was in vain as the team began to loaf.
   (Write the words with long "o," long "a," and long "e" sounds.)

   ____

5. I will spread butter on the bread.
   (Write the words with short "e" sounds.)

   ____

6. The feather from the dead eagle lay on the beach.
   (Write the words with short "e," long "e," and long "a" sounds.)

   ____

7. A frail male rode the mule.
   (Write the words with long "a," long "o," and long "u" sounds.)

   ____

8. The dainty queen broached the subject.
   (Write the words with long "a," long "o," and long "e" sounds.)

   ____

9. The wool from the wee sheep will be used to make tweed.
   (Write the words with long "e" and silent "e" sounds.)

   ____

10. Beef is the meat to braise or roast.
    (Write the words with long "e," long "a," and long "o" sounds.)

    ____

Name: ______________________________ Date: ________________

Learning About Words With the Vowel Pairs "ei," "ie," and "ey": *Learning About the "ei" Vowel Pair*

In many words that have a vowel combination, the first vowel is given the long sound and the second vowel is silent. In some words, the vowel sound is short rather than long. The best way to determine the sound of these vowel combinations is to determine if the word in which the vowel combination is found makes sense in a sentence. If it doesn't, try the other sound to see if the new word makes sense.

The vowel pair "ei" is found in many words. In the words below the vowels "ei" will have the long sound of "e" as in *either* or the long "a" sound like "ei" in *eight.*

Example: **ei**ther = long "e" sound **Example**: **ei**ght = long "a" sound

In each of the following sentences, the words with the "ei" vowels have the long sound of "e" or the long sound of "a." Read the sentences and determine the sound of the vowel pair. Place the word on the blank to show the sound of "ei." The first one has been completed for you. **Hint**: If you don't know how to pronounce a word, try both the long "e" and long "a" sound to see if either sound is a word you know.

	ei Word	Long e	Long a
1. Neither John nor Sam went to the game.	neither	e	___
2. The woman with the beige hat sat quietly.	________	___	___
3. We spent our leisure time jogging.	________	___	___
4. If war starts, they will seize the island.	________	___	___
5. The freight will arrive by truck.	________	___	___

Write a sentence using each of the following "ei" words. Also, complete the blanks to show the sound of "ei."

1. **protein** long ___
   Sentence: ____
2. **neighbor** long ___
   Sentence: ____
3. **conceive** long ___
   Sentence: ____
4. **rein** long ___
   Sentence: ____
5. **sleigh** long ___
   Sentence: ____

Name: ______________________ Date: ______________

Learning About Words With the Vowel Pairs "ei," "ie," and "ey": *Learning About the "ie" Vowel Pair*

The "ie" vowel pair has the long "i" or long "e" sound in the word.

> **Example**: The long sound of "i" is found in the word "die."
> **Example**: The long sound of "e" is found in the word "field."

In each of the following sentences is a word with the "ie" vowel pair. Read each sentence and determine the sound of the "ie" pair. Complete the blanks. The first one has been completed for you. **Hint**: If you don't know how to pronounce a word, try both the long "i" and long "e" sound. See which sound gives a word you know.

		ie Word	Long i	Long e
1.	The chief was at the fire station.	chief	____	e
2.	He tried to complete the homework.	________	____	____
3.	They have not replied to our letter.	________	____	____
4.	Will they send relief supplies to help?	________	____	____
5.	Practice good hygiene by washing your hands.	________	____	____
6.	Rabies is common among wild animals.	________	____	____

Write a sentence using each of the following "ie" words. Also, complete the blanks to show the sound of "ie."

1. **piece** long ____
   Sentence: ________________________________
2. **pried** long ____
   Sentence: ________________________________
3. **achieve** long ____
   Sentence: ________________________________
4. **spies** long ____
   Sentence: ________________________________
5. **shriek** long ____
   Sentence: ________________________________
6. **dried** long ____
   Sentence: ________________________________

Name: ______________________________ Date: ____________________

Learning About Words With the Vowel Pairs "ei," "ie," and "ey": *Learning About the "ey" Vowel Pair*

In some words, the letter combination "ey" has a long "e" sound. In other words, the "ey" makes the long "a" sound.

Example: donk**ey** = long "e" sound **Example**: h**ey** = long "a" sound

Read each of the following sentences and circle the word with the "ey" vowel pair. Then place a check mark to indicate the vowel sound of the "ey" vowel pair. **Hint**: If a word doesn't make sense using one long sound, try the other long sound.

1. In the west, they grow a grain called barley. ___ long e ___ long a
2. Many people now raise bees and sell the honey. ___ long e ___ long a
3. Do you have enough money for the movie? ___ long e ___ long a
4. Cats prey on mice. ___ long e ___ long a
5. The monkey was kept in a cage. ___ long e ___ long a
6. Marco Polo's journey to China took many years. ___ long e ___ long a
7. The winning jockey in the race was a woman. ___ long e ___ long a
8. You must obey the rules in school. ___ long e ___ long a
9. The glee club sang a medley of songs. ___ long e ___ long a
10. Meals are prepared in the galley of the ship. ___ long e ___ long a

Write a sentence using each of the following "ey" words. Also, complete the blanks to show the sound of "ey."

1. **hockey** long ___
   Sentence: ______________________________
2. **hey** long ___
   Sentence: ______________________________
3. **they** long ___
   Sentence: ______________________________
4. **kidney** long ___
   Sentence: ______________________________
5. **convey** long ___
   Sentence: ______________________________

Name: ______________________________ Date: ____________________

Learning About Words With the Vowel Pairs "ei," "ie," and "ey": *Reviewing What Has Been Learned About "ei," "ie," "ay," and "ey"*

In each of the following sentences is a blank. Unscramble the letters at the end of each sentence to make a word with the vowel pair "ei," "ie," "ay," or "ey." Write the word on the blank to make a meaningful sentence. Then write what vowel sound the vowel pair makes.

Vowel Sound

1. Golf is a ____________ time sport. **eislreu** ____________
2. Bears love to eat ____________. **yonhe** ____________
3. In the Civil War, there were many ____________. **pises** ____________
4. Each of us must ____________ opportunities. **eizes** ____________
5. To win we must ____________ well. **layp** ____________
6. The sunny day gave us a ____________ of hope. **yra** ____________
7. The ____________ is a beast of burden. **kednoy** ____________
8. We should ____________ the package soon. **eievrce** ____________
9. The ____________ was a kind man. **riepts** ____________
10. Do you ____________ his story? **elibeve** ____________
11. Roman soldiers carried a ____________. **hsldie** ____________
12. She wore a ____________ skirt. **eigbe** ____________
13. After it snowed, we went for a ____________ ride. **lsiehg** ____________
14. We must try hard to ____________ our goal. **chievae** ____________
15. The sailor ____________ the rope to the wharf. **edit** ____________
16. ____________, where do you think you are going? **eyh** ____________
17. What was the winning time in the ____________ race? **leray** ____________
18. Mom's apple ____________ were the best at the fair. **sipe** ____________
19. Our ____________ just trimmed his bushes. **ghnbroei** ____________
20. The jewelry was stolen by a ____________. **itehf** ____________

Name: ______________________________ Date: ____________________

Learning About "oo," "au," "aw," and "ew": *Learning about the "oo" Vowel Pair*

The vowel pairs "oo," "au," "aw," and "ew" are found in many words. When these vowel pairs are found in a word, the sound is neither long or short.

In many words with the vowel pair "oo," the "oo" is sounded like "oo" in *boot.* In other words, the "oo" is sounded like the "oo" in *good.* Pronounce each of the following words aloud. Watch carefully how you make the "oo" sound. If the "oo" sounds like "oo" in *good,* place the word on a blank under **good**. If the "oo" sound like the "oo" in *boot,* place the word on a blank under **boot**.

roof	**root**	**book**	**shoot**	**spoon**	**nook**	**shook**
crook	**doom**	**room**	**poor**	**tooth**	**hoof**	**food**
cook	**noon**	**pool**	**loop**			

boot		**good**	
____________	____________	____________	____________
____________	____________	____________	____________
____________	____________	____________	____________
____________	____________	____________	____________
____________	____________	____________	____________

Match each of the following words with the definition on the right.

_____ 1. nook a. sound made by a train or ship

_____ 2. brood b. sailing vessel

_____ 3. moor c. produced by sheep

_____ 4. toot d. land of poor drainage and wasteland in England

_____ 5. gloom e. chess piece

_____ 6. hoop f. number of small animals hatched at same time

_____ 7. rook g. a corner in a room

_____ 8. brook h. feeling of sadness

_____ 9. sloop i. small stream

_____ 10. wool j. circular band of metal or wood

Name: ______________________________ Date: ____________________

Learning About "oo," "au," "aw," and "ew": *Using "oo" Words in Sentences*

Complete the blanks in each of the following sentences using the words below.

brook gloom nook brood cool rook moor wool sloop toot

1. In England the ______________ is a land of poor drainage and wasteland.
2. She played the ______________ well and won the chess game.
3. A mother duck and her ______________ waddled toward the lake.
4. The ______________ breeze brought relief from the heat.
5. The bad news resulted in a feeling of ______________ by all.
6. When we heard the ______________ of the train whistle, we were sad.
7. Although the room was large, they had only a ______________ for their own use.
8. We camped by a small mountain ______________ that bubbled and gurgled all night.
9. The ______________ from the sheep will be used to make shirts.
10. Late at night, the ______________ quietly sailed into the open sea.

Use one of the following consonants in each blank to make a word that completes the meaning of the sentence.

sch b sm l h m sh sp g n sl bl br w r c cr tr st

1. The flowers by the ___ ___ook will ___ ___oom in the fall.
2. By the creek was the ___oof print left by the ___oose.
3. The ___ ___ool of ___ool will be used to make a shirt.
4. They wrote a ___ook about the ___oose who was ___oose.
5. In the ___ook of the ___oom he sat by himself.
6. He went to ___ ___ ___ool to learn how to make ___ookies.
7. A ___ ___ooth ___ ___ook is hard to catch.
8. When the bugle sounded, the ___ ___oop ___ ___ood ready for inspection.
9. Across the ___oor a ___ool breeze blew.
10. The ___ ___oop ___ ___ook as it began to sail out to sea.

Name: ______________________________ Date: ____________________

Learning About "oo," "au," "aw," and "ew": *Reviewing What Has Been Learned*

Read each of the following sentences. Follow the directions for each sentence. Write a sentence using the words written on the blanks.

1. I looked through the pane and saw a lame moose. (Write the words with a silent "e".)

   ____

   Sentence: ______________________________

   Sentence: ______________________________

   Sentence: ______________________________

2. The animal with a white stripe left a vile smell. (Write the words with a silent "e" and a long "i" sound.)

   ____

   Sentence: ______________________________

   Sentence: ______________________________

   Sentence: ______________________________

3. On the throne in a robe sat the king with a phone. (Write the words with a long "o" and a silent "e".)

   ____

   Sentence: ______________________________

   Sentence: ______________________________

   Sentence: ______________________________

4. A dude with a flute played a tune. (Write the words with a long "u" and a silent "e".)

   ____

   Sentence: ______________________________

   Sentence: ______________________________

   Sentence: ______________________________

5. In the chaise rode a frail maid. (Write the words with "ai" and a long "a" sound.)

   ____

   Sentence: ______________________________

   Sentence: ______________________________

   Sentence: ______________________________

Name: ______________________________ Date: ____________________

Learning About "oo," "au," "aw," and "ew": *Reviewing What Has Been Learned (continued)*

6. The dray was loaded with gray clay. (Write the words with "ay" and a long "a" sound.)

   ____

   Sentence: ____
   Sentence: ____
   Sentence: ____

7. The bleach left a streak on the pleat. (Write the words with "ea" and a long "e" sound.)

   ____

   Sentence: ____
   Sentence: ____
   Sentence: ____

8. Tweed is made from the fleece of a sheep. (Write the words with "ee" and a long "e" sound.)

   ____

   Sentence: ____
   Sentence: ____
   Sentence: ____

9. The goal was to coax a moan from the goat. (Write the words with "oa" and a long "o" sound.)

   ____

   Sentence: ____
   Sentence: ____
   Sentence: ____
   Sentence: ____

10. In the zoo a goose stood on one foot by the pool. (Write the words with the "oo" sound under the words "doom" or "hook" below with the same "oo" sound.)

doom	**hook**
____________	____________
____________	____________
____________	

Name: ______________________________ Date: ____________________

Learning About "oo," "au," "aw," and "ew": *Learning About "au" and "aw" Words*

The letter pairs "au" and "aw" are found in many words. These two letter pairs make the sound "aw" in words where they are found. The following are some words with the "au" or "aw" letter pairs.

Complete the blank in each sentence using a word from the list below.

applause shawl brawl launch caustic prawn thaw laundry gauze caw

1. They plan to ________________ the rocket today.
2. She wore a blue ________________ around her shoulders
3. It was so warm we were afraid the ice would ________________.
4. A ________________ is not a sign of manhood.
5. His ________________ remarks hurt my feelings.
6. Another word for shrimp is ________________.
7. We had to do our ________________ before leaving on the trip.
8. The speaker knew the crowd was pleased when the ________________ went on for five minutes.
9. In case there is an accident, we will take tape and ________________ on our camping trip.
10. The ________________ from the crow frightened the other animals.

Unscramble the following letters to make a word with the letter pair "au" or "aw." Use the word in a sentence.

1. untag ________________
   Sentence: ____
2. ttnau ________________
   Sentence: ____
3. aldrw ________________
   Sentence: ____
4. npswa ________________
   Sentence: ____
5. rudfa ________________
   Sentence: ____

Name: ______________________ Date: ______________

Learning About "oo," "au," "aw," and "ew": *Learning About "ew" Words*

Read each of the following sentences. Circle the word in parentheses that best completes the sentence.

1. The (crew / crow) from the ship was on time.
2. The wind (blow / blew) all day.
3. You should (chow / chew) your food carefully.
4. We will have (stew / stow) for lunch.
5. Their homework was to (brew / draw) their favorite pet.
6. We could not mow the lawn until the (few / dew) dried.
7. She (throw / threw) the pitch that won the game.
8. In the church we sat in a (dew / pew).
9. The bird (flew / clew) away before I could take the picture.
10. Mother said she would (crew / brew) the coffee.

Unscramble each of the sets of letters to make a word with the letter pair "ew." Write the words made on the blank by the definitions below.

1. Benchlike seat in church ______________ wpe
2. To go over something again ______________ ewriev
3. A combination of meat and vegetables ______________ tswe
4. Sound made by a cat ______________ wem
5. Moisture found on the ground in the morning ______________ wde
6. Name of a salamander ______________ wnet
7. An evergreen tree ______________ wey
8. Mouselike animal with long snout ______________ hrwse
9. To scatter over a wide area ______________ rtews
10. A valuable material ______________ wejel

Name: ______________________ Date: ______________

Learning About Words With Inflectional Endings: *Adding "ing" to Words That End in a Consonant*

Many words end with "ed" or "ing." To add "ed" or "ing" to words ending with a single consonant, you usually double the last consonant and then add "ed" or "ing."

Complete each of the following blanks and make a new word by adding "ing" to the base word. Read the sentence and complete the blank using the base word correctly.

	Base Word	Double the Final Consonant	Add "ing" to Make the New Word
1.	**dig**	__ __ __ __	__ __ __ __ __ __ __
	When the rain came we stopped ____________ in the garden.		
2.	**cut**	__ __ __ __	__ __ __ __ __ __ __
	We were ____________ the weeds when the rain began.		
3.	**sit**	__ __ __ __	__ __ __ __ __ __ __
	The old man was ____________ by the roadside.		
4.	**lug**	__ __ __ __	__ __ __ __ __ __ __
	They were ____________ the sled loaded with groceries up the hill.		
5.	**fan**	__ __ __ __	__ __ __ __ __ __ __
	The people were ____________ themselves in the hot theater.		
6.	**nag**	__ __ __ __	__ __ __ __ __ __ __
	The little boy was ____________ his mother for more candy.		
7.	**chop**	__ __ __ __ __	__ __ __ __ __ __ __ __
	____________ wood is great exercise but very hard work.		
8.	**run**	__ __ __ __	__ __ __ __ __ __ __
	The girl went ____________ every day at 4:00.		
9.	**tan**	__ __ __ __	__ __ __ __ __ __ __
	In early America, ____________ skins to make shoes was very common.		
10.	**shop**	__ __ __ __ __	__ __ __ __ __ __ __ __
	It seems that many people never tire from ____________.		

Name: ______________________________ Date: ____________________

Learning About Words With Inflectional Endings: *Adding "ed" to Words That End in a Consonant*

Complete the following blanks and make a new word by adding "ed" to the base word. Read the sentence and complete the blank using the base word correctly.

	Base Word	Double the Final Consonant	Add "ed" to Make the New Word
1.	**beg**	__ __ __ __	__ __ __ __ __ __

The little boy ________________ his father for more money.

2.	**bat**	__ __ __ __	__ __ __ __ __ __

She ________________ the ball across the fence in left field

3.	**stop**	__ __ __ __ __	__ __ __ __ __ __ __

The old man ________________ and sat by the roadside to rest.

4.	**lug**	__ __ __ __	__ __ __ __ __ __

They ________________ the sled loaded with groceries up the hill

5.	**dim**	__ __ __ __	__ __ __ __ __ __

He ________________ the lights as the other car came into view.

6.	**nag**	__ __ __ __	__ __ __ __ __ __

The little boy ________________ his mother for more candy

7.	**chop**	__ __ __ __ __	__ __ __ __ __ __ __

He ________________ wood to get in shape for football.

8.	**stun**	__ __ __ __ __	__ __ __ __ __ __ __

The town was ________________ when the tornado struck.

9.	**tan**	__ __ __ __	__ __ __ __ __ __

They came back from vacation ________________ and rested.

10.	**trot**	__ __ __ __ __	__ __ __ __ __ __ __

The young colt ________________ by the side of its mother.

Name: ______________________________ Date: ____________________

Learning About Words With Inflectional Endings: *Reviewing "ing" and "ed"*

Complete the blank in each of the following sentences by adding either "ing" or "ed" to the words on the right.

1. They ______________ us for sleeping so late. **kid**
2. She is ______________ holes to plant roses. **dig**
3. The boys were ______________ along the beach. **jog**
4. We ______________ the floor yesterday. **mop**
5. Yesterday she ______________ briefly after lunch. **nap**
6. He is ______________ to complete his homework before class. **plan**
7. The ______________ of many fur-bearing animals is against the law. **trap**
8. When he began ______________ the lights, it became hard to read. **dim**
9. After watching for hours, he ______________ a bald eagle. **spot**
10. In many national forests, ______________ of the trees is not permitted. **log**

Name: ______________________________ Date: ____________________

Learning About Words With Inflectional Endings: *Adding “ing” to Words Ending in Silent “e”*

When adding “ing” to a word that ends in silent “e,” first drop the silent “e” and then add “ing” to make a new word.

Example: ride = **rid** + **ing** = riding

Complete the blanks below to make a new word with “ing.” Write a sentence using the new word.

	Base Word	Drop the Silent “e”	Add “ing” to Make the New Word
1.	**quake**	_ _ _ _	_ _ _ _ _ _ _
2.	**strive**	_ _ _ _ _	_ _ _ _ _ _ _ _
3.	**thrive**	_ _ _ _ _	_ _ _ _ _ _ _ _
4.	**evade**	_ _ _ _	_ _ _ _ _ _ _
5.	**hone**	_ _ _	_ _ _ _ _ _
6.	**fume**	_ _ _	_ _ _ _ _ _
7.	**clone**	_ _ _ _	_ _ _ _ _ _ _
8.	**shame**	_ _ _ _	_ _ _ _ _ _ _
9.	**drone**	_ _ _ _	_ _ _ _ _ _ _
10.	**mime**	_ _ _	_ _ _ _ _ _

Each item is followed by: Sentence: ______________________________

Name: ______________________ Date: ______________

Learning About Words With Inflectional Endings: *Adding "ing" to Words Ending in Silent "e" (continued)*

Complete each of the following sentences by adding "ing" to the words below. Write the correct word with the "ing" ending on the blank in the sentence.

arrive	**advise**	**spruce**	**choose**	**stoke**
probe	**glaze**	**evade**	**file**	**fumble**

1. They will be ______________ this afternoon by plane.
2. We were late to school, so we are ______________ the principal.
3. To make sure the records are complete, the teachers are ______________ all grade reports.
4. The city workers were ______________ up the park before summer.
5. He kept ______________ the ball, and it cost our team the game.
6. She is at the paint store ______________ colors for the room.
7. Scientists are ______________ the universe for signs of other civilizations.
8. They are ______________ the wall with a thin coat of paint.
9. One of the jobs of teachers is ______________ new students.
10. While camping, we spent the night ______________ the fire.

Name: ________________________ Date: ________________

Learning About Words With Inflectional Endings: *Adding "ing" to Words Ending in "y"*

To add "ing" to words ending with the letter "y," just add "ing" to the end of the word.

Example: fry = frying cry = crying

Complete each of the following blanks and make a new word by adding "ing." Use each word in a sentence.

	Base Word	**Add "ing" to Make the New Word**
1.	**jockey**	__ __ __ __ __ __ __ __ __
	Sentence: ____________________	
2.	**fancy**	__ __ __ __ __ __ __ __
	Sentence: ____________________	
3.	**hurry**	__ __ __ __ __ __ __ __
	Sentence: ____________________	
4.	**pry**	__ __ __ __ __ __
	Sentence: ____________________	
5.	**scurry**	__ __ __ __ __ __ __ __ __
	Sentence: ____________________	
6.	**curry**	__ __ __ __ __ __ __ __
	Sentence: ____________________	
7.	**multiply**	__ __ __ __ __ __ __ __ __ __ __
	Sentence: ____________________	
8.	**study**	__ __ __ __ __ __ __ __
	Sentence: ____________________	
9.	**journey**	__ __ __ __ __ __ __ __ __ __
	Sentence: ____________________	
10.	**survey**	__ __ __ __ __ __ __ __ __
	Sentence: ____________________	

Name: ______________________________ Date: ________________

Learning About Words With Inflectional Endings: *Learning to Use "s" and "es" to Form Plurals*

An "s" or "es" is added to the singular form of a word to make the word plural. **Singular** means one. **Plural** means more than one.

Example: car = singular cars = plural
box = singular boxes = plural

Each of the following words is singular or plural. Complete each sentence below using one of the words. Place a check on the proper blank to show if the word in the blank is singular or plural.

beach	**boy**	**team**	**girl**	**frogs**
beaches	**peach**	**church**	**teams**	**foxes**
churches	**dresses**	**boys**	**dishes**	**dress**

	Singular	Plural
1. The three ________________ are leaving for camp.	____	____
2. In old England, ________________ were hunted for sport.	____	____
3. Each ________________ plans to try out for the girls' soccer team.	____	____
4. Both ________________ are on the field ready to play.	____	____
5. The members of each ________________ are wearing their school colors.	____	____
6. He was the only ________________ planning to go on the trip.	____	____
7. We plan to attend ________________ on Sunday morning.	____	____
8. She has some very pretty ________________.	____	____
9. In the pond were many ________________ whose croaking kept us awake.	____	____
10. This Sunday there will be a celebration at ten different ________________.	____	____
11. She decided to wear her blue ________________.	____	____
12. We put the ________________ in the dishwasher.	____	____
13. In World War II, soldiers landed on many ________________.	____	____
14. I plan to spend the day at the ________________.	____	____
15. He brought a ________________ for lunch.	____	____

Name: ______________________________ Date: ____________________

Learning About Words With Inflectional Endings: *Forming the Plural of Words Ending in "y" With a Consonant Before the "y"*

All of the following words end in "y" with a consonant coming before the "y." To change such words to the plural form, first change the "y" to "i" and then add "es."

Example: Fly ends in "y" and the consonant "l" comes before the "y"
Change the "y" to "i" and add "es" fly = flies

Change each of these words in Column I to a word that ends in "ies." Write the new word on the blank under Column II. Write a sentence using the plural form.

	Singular Form	Changed to Plural Form by	Plural Form
1.	**factory**	changing ___ to ___ and adding ___ ___	____________
	Sentence: ________________________________		
2.	**memory**	changing ___ to ___ and adding ___ ___	____________
	Sentence: ________________________________		
3.	**twenty**	changing ___ to ___ and adding ___ ___	____________
	Sentence: ________________________________		
4.	**county**	changing ___ to ___ and adding ___ ___	____________
	Sentence: ________________________________		
5.	**poppy**	changing ___ to ___ and adding ___ ___	____________
	Sentence: ________________________________		
6.	**fancy**	changing ___ to ___ and adding ___ ___	____________
	Sentence: ________________________________		
7.	**surgery**	changing ___ to ___ and adding ___ ___	____________
	Sentence: ________________________________		
8.	**study**	changing ___ to ___ and adding ___ ___	____________
	Sentence: ________________________________		
9.	**navy**	changing ___ to ___ and adding ___ ___	____________
	Sentence: ________________________________		
10.	**party**	changing ___ to ___ and adding ___ ___	____________
	Sentence: ________________________________		

Name: ______________________________ Date: ______________

Learning About Words With Inflectional Endings: *Forming the Plural of Words Ending in "o"*

For many words ending in "o" following a consonant, the plural is formed by adding "es."

Example: potato = potatoes

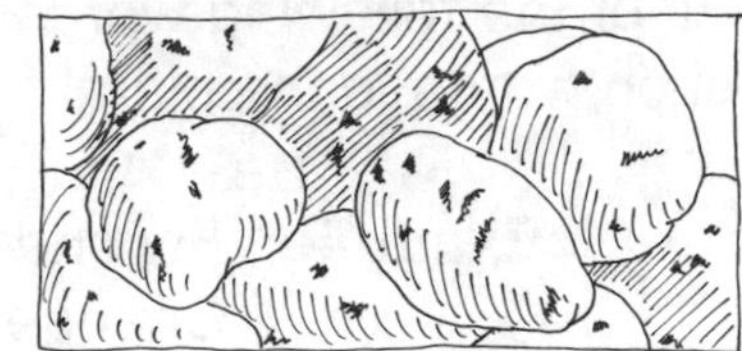

Words that end in "o" following a vowel form the plural by adding "s."

Example: rodeo = rodeos

Find the singular word from Column III that matches the definitions in Column I. Write the singular or plural form of the word that matches the definition on the blank under Column II.

	Column I	Column II	Column III
1.	a vegetable that is red when ripe	____________	**Eskimo**
2.	ten very brave soldiers	____________	**tomato**
3.	five sure-footed pack animals	____________	**rodeo**
4.	where cowboys perform on horses	____________	**zero**
5.	the number one million has six	____________	**burro**
6.	they are good when fried or baked	____________	**shampoo**
7.	you always find them on the highway	____________	**potato**
8.	a song sung by one person	____________	**piano**
9.	family albums have many	____________	**solo**
10.	a musical instrument	____________	**photo**
11.	many of these animals are in Australia	____________	**radio**
12.	what one does to the hair	____________	**auto**
13.	what happens to sound in the mountains	____________	**kangaroo**
14.	they live north of the Arctic Circle	____________	**hero**
15.	an electronic music box	____________	**echo**

Name: ______________________ Date: ______________

Learning About Words With Inflectional Endings: *Adding "er" to Words Ending in "y"*

When you need to add "er" to a word that ends in a consonant and "y" to make a comparison word, first change the "y" to "i" and then add "er."

Example: muddy = muddier

In the sentences below, a word is in bold. Change the word in bold to a word ending in "er." Write a new sentence using the "er" word.

"er" form

1. Mums are a **hardy** flower. ______________
   Sentence: ______________________________
2. This is a **lively** dance. ______________
   Sentence: ______________________________
3. He wore a **fancy** pair of new shoes. ______________
   Sentence: ______________________________
4. There is a **tiny** man by the phone book. ______________
   Sentence: ______________________________
5. She drew a **funny** face on her notebook. ______________
   Sentence: ______________________________
6. The big granite rock was **heavy**. ______________
   Sentence: ______________________________
7. The river was **muddy** after the two inch rain. ______________
   Sentence: ______________________________
8. The picture on the wall was very **pretty**. ______________
   Sentence: ______________________________
9. Summer is the **busy** season for many people. ______________
   Sentence: ______________________________
10. The road we took to the top of the mountain was **rocky**. ______________
    Sentence: ______________________________

Name: ______________________________ Date: ____________________

Learning About Words With Inflectional Endings: *Adding "est" to Words Ending in "y"*

To add "est" to a word ending in a consonant and the letter "y," first change the "y" to an "i" and then add "est."

In the sentences below, a word is in bold that ends in "y." In each word, a consonant comes before the "y." Make a new word by changing the "y" to "i" and adding "est." Place the new word on the blank following each sentence. Write a sentence using the new "est" word.

"est" word

1. He is **happy** now that his friends are back. ____________

   Sentence: ______________________________

2. They told some very **funny** stories. ____________

   Sentence: ______________________________

3. She decided to buy the **pretty** blue skirt. ____________

   Sentence: ______________________________

4. He left the **muddy** pair of boots by the door. ____________

   Sentence: ______________________________

5. I think math is **easy** in the first hour class. ____________

   Sentence: ______________________________

6. He is **grumpy** in the morning. ____________

   Sentence: ______________________________

7. The big truck carries a **heavy** load. ____________

   Sentence: ______________________________

8. He caught an **ugly** catfish and a beautiful trout. ____________

   Sentence: ______________________________

9. Many **hardy** wildflowers are in need of rain. ____________

   Sentence: ______________________________

Name: ______________________________ Date: ________________

Learning About Words With Inflectional Endings: *Adding "er" and "est" to Make New Words*

Add "er" and "est" to each of the base words to make new words. Write the "er" and "est" words on the appropriate blanks.

	Base Word	Base Word + "er"	Base Word + "est"
1.	smooth	____________	____________
2.	clean	____________	____________
3.	high	____________	____________
4.	fast	____________	____________
5.	light	____________	____________
6.	low	____________	____________
7.	sharp	____________	____________
8.	strong	____________	____________
9.	cold	____________	____________
10.	bright	____________	____________

Each of the following words ends with a consonant with a vowel before the consonant. Double the consonant and add "er" and "est" to each of the base words. Write the "er" and "est" words on the blanks.

	Base Word	Base Word + "er"	Base Word + "est"
1.	hot	____________	____________
2.	sad	____________	____________
3.	fat	____________	____________
4.	mad	____________	____________
5.	flat	____________	____________
6.	wet	____________	____________
7.	fit	____________	____________
8.	red	____________	____________

Name: ______________________________ Date: ____________________

Learning About Words With Inflectional Endings: *Adding "s" and "ed" to Make New Words*

Many new words can be made by adding "s" or "ed" to a word. Complete the blanks in each sentence by adding "s" or "ed" to the base word.

1. **walk** (a) He ______________ home from school yesterday.
   (b) She ______________ home from school every day.
2. **shout** (a) We heard the ______________ of distress from across the lake.
   (b) He became angry and ______________ at the official.
3. **wait** (a) I wonder if they ______________ until the mail was all delivered?
   (b) She gets up early each morning and ______________ for a phone call.
4. **coast** (a) They took their sled and ______________ until dark.
   (b) Many of the ______________ along the North Sea are summer vacation spots.
5. **hoist** (a) The team ______________ the coach on their shoulders after winning a game.
   (b) Yesterday he ______________ the large rock above his head.
6. **flaunt** (a) He ______________ all of the new clothes his mother buys him.
   (b) They ______________ the news reports showing their great success.
7. **surround** (a) They have ______________ the wild horses in hopes of catching one.
   (b) When the team wins, the pep squad always ______________ the team and cheers.
8. **learn** (a) I hope he has ______________ a lesson from his bad experience.
   (b) He ______________ about animals when he goes to the zoo.
9. **clean** (a) He ______________ his desk every morning.
   (b) Every room was ______________ before we left for school.
10. **sprout** (a) Uncle John refers to young boys as young ______________.
    (b) The corn was planted two weeks before it ______________.

Name: ______________________________ Date: ____________________

Learning About Words With Inflectional Endings: *Learning About the Sounds of "ed"*

When the inflection "ed" is added to a base word, the "ed" may be sounded as **/ed/**, **/t/**, or **/d/**. When "ed" is added to a base word that ends in "d" or "t," the "ed" is sounded as **/ed/**.

Example: plant + ed = planted = /ed/ sound

When the inflection "ed" is added to a base word not ending in "d" or "t," the sound of "ed" may be **/d/** or **/t/**.

Examples: kick + ed = kicked = /t/ sound
fish + ed = fished = /d/ sound

Each sentence below has a word in bold. Read each of the sentences and write "ed," "t," or "d" on the blank above the inflection to show the correct sound of the inflection.

1. Many native American Indians lived in one area and **planted** corn each spring.
2. Many native American Indians **hunted** animals.
3. He **wanted** to make sure everyone was prepared for the test.
4. The band **played** for over an hour.
5. When he heard the noise, he **jumped** to his feet.
6. The principal said he **wished** the school year was longer.
7. The artist **painted** beautiful scenes while relaxing at the beach.
8. In early America, young people **worked** very hard.
9. During World War II, marines **landed** on the beaches of France.
10. In early America, all members of the family **helped** with the daily chores.

Name: ______________________ Date: ______________________

Learning About Words With Inflectional Endings: *Reviewing Inflections*

Each of the sentences has a word in bold followed by a blank. Write the correct form of the word on the blank below the word in bold. The first one has been completed for you.

1. The roses **plant**____ in the spring are blooming. We are now **plant**____ fall flowers.
   planted planting
2. We **hurry**____ to catch the train. When we got to the station others were **hurry**____ to catch the same train.
3. The **small**____ of the three brothers was ten years old. The other two brothers were **large**____.
4. The **hardy**____ flowers can stand cold weather. Some flowers are **hardy**____ than others.
5. In war, bridges and buildings are **destroy**____. War often **destroy**____ the history of a people.
6. Many of the people were on the streets where they **beg**____ for food. Some of those **beg**____ were homeless.
7. The band included seven **flute**____ and two **piano**____.
8. Ten seventh-grade **girl**____ made the soccer team that plays today. The **play**____ from both teams will be introduced before the game.
9. John is the **slow**____ of the two runners. He is not the **slow**____ runner on the track team.
10. The cook was **fry**____ the potatoes. Everyone was wanting french **fry**____.

Name: ______________________ Date: ______________

Learning About Compound Words: *Finding Root Words in Compound Words*

Compound words are words that include two root words. For example, the root words **any** and **one** form the compound word **anyone**.

Example: out + side = outside home + town = hometown

Each of the following words is a compound word. Write the root words on the blanks. Then write a sentence using the compound word. The first one has been partially completed for you.

	Compound Word	Root Word	Root Word
1.	**alongside**	along	side
	Sentence: ______________________		
2.	**framework**	________	________
	Sentence: ______________________		
3.	**everything**	________	________
	Sentence: ______________________		
4.	**mainland**	________	________
	Sentence: ______________________		
5.	**downstream**	________	________
	Sentence: ______________________		
6.	**furthermore**	________	________
	Sentence: ______________________		
7.	**commonplace**	________	________
	Sentence: ______________________		
8.	**boldface**	________	________
	Sentence: ______________________		
9.	**businessmen**	________	________
	Sentence: ______________________		
10.	**farewell**	________	________
	Sentence: ______________________		

Name: ______________________________ Date: ______________

Learning About Compound Words: *Finding Compound Words in Sentences*

Each of the following sentences contains one or more compound words. Underline the compound words and write the roots on the blanks after the sentence.

	Root 1	Root 2
1. The goldfish must not be fed too much food.	________	________
2. When the new school is built, sandstone will be used for the foundation.	________	________
3. Be sure to clean the room, otherwise we will be late getting away.	________	________
4. We must make sure that eating a balanced meal is widespread.	________	________
5. Many townspeople were without the needed protection from the storm.	________ ________	________ ________
6. Everybody thought the quarterback should pass more.	________ ________	________ ________
7. The newspaper reported that the homework was common.	________ ________	________ ________
8. In the schoolhouse were many textbooks that were for classroom use only.	________ ________ ________	________ ________ ________
9. The summertime thunderstorm came from the southeast.	________ ________ ________	________ ________ ________
10. Many cowboys dressed in buckskin whenever they were on the range.	________ ________ ________	________ ________ ________

Name: ______________________________ Date: ____________________

Learning About Compound Words: *Making Compound Words From Root Words*

Make compound words using the words from Column I in the first position joined with the words from Column II in the last position. Write the compound words on the blanks under Column III.

Column I	Column II	Column III
rattle	cob	1. ____________
foot	stick	2. ____________
corn	spout	3. ____________
cat	snake	4. ____________
row	way	5. ____________
note	bath	6. ____________
tree	fish	7. ____________
no	saw	8. ____________
hour	flow	9. ____________
bird	print	10. ____________
hall	nail	11. ____________
see	current	12. ____________
water	book	13. ____________
over	house	14. ____________
under	glass	15. ____________
finger	body	16. ____________
yard	boat	17. ____________

Name: ______________________________ Date: ________________

Learning About Compound Words: *Using Compound Words in Sentences*

Use each of the following compound words in a sentence.

1. **airline** Sentence: ______________________________
____
2. **steamboat** Sentence: ______________________________
____
3. **textbook** Sentence: ______________________________
____
4. **flagpole** Sentence: ______________________________
____
5. **vineyard** Sentence: ______________________________
____
6. **classroom** Sentence: ______________________________
____
7. **stagecoach** Sentence: ______________________________
____
8. **handshake** Sentence: ______________________________
____
9. **classmate** Sentence: ______________________________
____
10. **seaport** Sentence: ______________________________
____

Name: ______________________________ Date: ____________________

Learning About Compound Words: *Unscrambling Letters to Make Compound Words*

Use the letters on the right to make a compound word. Write a sentence using the compound word.

1. ______________ oughrasls

   Sentence: ______________________________

2. ______________ nligoomht

   Sentence: ______________________________

3. ______________ earfllwe

   Sentence: ______________________________

4. ______________ estoimme

   Sentence: ______________________________

5. ______________ eeknwed

   Sentence: ______________________________

6. ______________ alnghiftl

   Sentence: ______________________________

7. ______________ erbwoye

   Sentence: ______________________________

8. ______________ arbkcyad

   Sentence: ______________________________

9. ______________ potrtee

   Sentence: ______________________________

10. ______________ unrseis

    Sentence: ______________________________

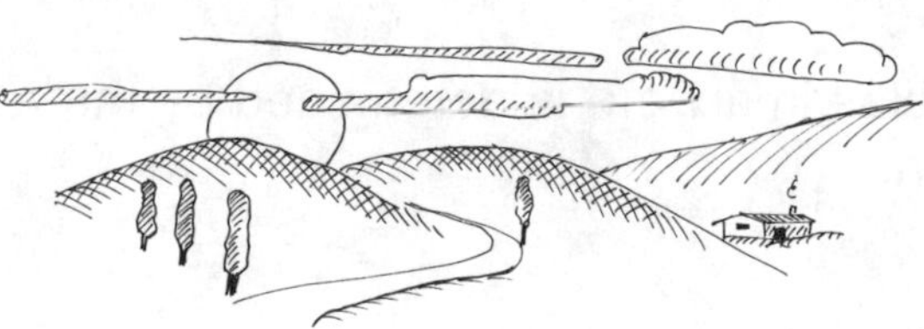

Name: ______________________________ Date: ____________________

Learning to Find the Syllables in Words: *Identifying the Vowel Sounds Heard in Words*

The number of **syllables** in a word is determined by the number of vowel sounds heard when a word is pronounced. Many words have more vowels than are heard when a word is pronounced.

Write the number of vowels seen in each word on the blank following each word. Each word has **one** syllable. The first one has been completed for you.

	Vowels Seen	Vowels Heard	Vowel Sound
1. paint	2	1	long a
2. rack	____	____	________
3. been	____	____	________
4. main	____	____	________
5. spring	____	____	________
6. ream	____	____	________
7. stake	____	____	________
8. treat	____	____	________
9. flake	____	____	________
10. field	____	____	________

11. In the words (a)__________, (b) __________, (c) __________, (d) __________, (e) __________, (f) __________, g) __________, and h) __________ two vowels are seen but only (i) __________ is heard when the word is pronounced.

12. In the words (a) __________ and (b) __________ one vowel is seen and (c) __________ vowel sound is heard.

Rule: The number of syllables in a word is determined by the number of vowel sounds **heard**, not the number seen.

Name: ______________________ Date: ______________

Learning to Find the Syllables in Words: *Finding the Number of Vowel Sounds in Words*

Pronounce each of the following words. Complete the blanks under each column.

Word	Vowels Seen	Vowels Heard	Number of Syllables
1. sit	_____	_____	_____
2. site	_____	_____	_____
3. mat	_____	_____	_____
4. mate	_____	_____	_____
5. razor	_____	_____	_____
6. welcome	_____	_____	_____
7. minor	_____	_____	_____
8. umpire	_____	_____	_____
9. faint	_____	_____	_____
10. feat	_____	_____	_____
11. plastic	_____	_____	_____
12. muzzle	_____	_____	_____
13. repeat	_____	_____	_____
14. extreme	_____	_____	_____
15. furnace	_____	_____	_____
16. please	_____	_____	_____
17. steering	_____	_____	_____
18. develop	_____	_____	_____
19. construction	_____	_____	_____
20. consideration	_____	_____	_____

Name: ____________________ Date: ______________

Learning to Find the Syllables in Words: *Learning About Open and Closed Syllables*

All words have one or more syllables. It will help you to pronounce unknown words if you know when a syllable is **open** or **closed**. In an open syllable the vowel sound is **usually** the long sound. In closed syllables the vowel sound is **usually** short. The spelling pattern for closed syllables is **cvc** or **consonant/vowel/consonant**. The spelling pattern for open syllables is **cv** or **consonant/vowel**.

Example: Closed syllable c/v/c cat **Example**: Open syllable c/v go

Each of the following words is a one-syllable word. Each is a closed- or open-syllable word. Pronounce each word and listen for the long or short vowel sound. If the vowel has a **short** sound, place the word under the Closed Syllable column. If the vowel sound has a **long** sound, place the word under the Open Syllable column.

so	**may**	**lie**	**dog**	**met**
man	**run**	**fan**	**me**	**see**
go	**say**	**be**	**mad**	**set**
tie	**bin**	**cap**	**big**	**ray**

Open Syllable	**Closed Syllable**
______________	______________
______________	______________
______________	______________
______________	______________
______________	______________
______________	______________
______________	______________
______________	______________
______________	______________
______________	______________

Name: ______________________________ Date: ____________________

Learning to Find the Syllables in Words: *Finding the Syllables in Two-Syllable Words*

When a two-syllable word is pronounced, two vowel sounds are heard.

Example: begin

When a word has a consonant between two vowels, the syllables are usually divided after the first vowel.

Example: be / gin The spelling pattern is cv/cvc (or cv/cv).

Divide each of the following words after the first vowel. Write the syllables on the blanks. Read the sentence that follows. The first one has been completed for you.

	Word	1st Syllable	Vowel (long/short)	2nd Syllable	Vowel (long/short/ silent/r-controlled)
1.	**bacon**	ba	long	con	short
	We had bacon for breakfast.				
2.	**below**	______	______	______	______
	The sailors went below deck.				
3.	**hobo**	______	______	______	______
	The hobo rode the train from city to city.				
4.	**hotel**	______	______	______	______
	We spent the evening at the hotel.				
5.	**local**	______	______	______	______
	Many local citizens were present.				
6.	**polite**	______	______	______	______
	We were told to be polite.				
7.	**vapor**	______	______	______	______
	The jet plane left a vapor trail in the sky.				
8.	**delay**	______	______	______	______
	It is important that we leave without delay.				
9.	**miser**	______	______	______	______
	The miser lived in a cave to save money.				
10.	**fatal**	______	______	______	______
	They made a fatal mistake that cost them the game.				

Name: ______________________________ Date: ____________________

Learning to Find the Syllables in Words: *Learning More About Open and Closed Syllables*

The words below are two-syllable words. Complete the blanks to show the open and closed syllables in each word. Show the long vowel sound by drawing a macron (¯) over the vowel. Show the short sound by drawing a breve (˘) over the vowel. Indicate the spelling pattern of each syllable as cv or cvc.

Word	Open Syllable	Spelling Pattern	Closed Syllable	Spelling Pattern
1. rival	________	____	________	____
2. demon	________	____	________	____
3. focus	________	____	________	____
4. label	________	____	________	____
5. bonus	________	____	________	____
6. human	________	____	________	____
7. lotus	________	____	________	____
8. final	________	____	________	____
9. minus	________	____	________	____
10. haven	________	____	________	____

Circle the correct answer to complete each statement.

11. In each of the above words, the open syllable has the spelling pattern:

    (a) cv (b) cvc

12. The vowel sound of the open syllable in the above words is:

    (a) long (b) short

13. In each of the above words, the closed syllable has the spelling pattern:

    (a) cv (b) cvc

14. The vowel sound of the closed syllable in the above words is:

    (a) long (b) short

Name: ______________________________ Date: ____________________

Learning to Find the Syllables in Words: *Learning That Spelling Patterns Don't Always Work*

Some words with the cvcv pattern do not divide after the first vowel. For example the word "robin" has a cvcv pattern. However, the word is divided between the "b" and "i."

Example: rob / in

In words like "robin" the first syllable is closed, so the vowel sound is the short sound.

In each of the following sentences, circle the word in parentheses that completes the meaning of the sentence. In some sentences, the first syllable is open. In others the first syllable is closed. Each word has a macron (long vowel sound) or breve (short vowel sound) to show the vowel sound of the first syllable.

1. In late winter a (rōbin / rŏbin) is a sign that spring is near.
2. The trip for the (vōcal / vŏcal) group will leave at noon.
3. How much (mōney / mŏney) will we need for the trip?
4. She wrote a (nōvel / nŏvel) about the Civil War.
5. He asked me to do a (fāvor / făvor) for him.
6. The (rāpid / răpid) end of the story suprised everyone.
7. She wore a (fāncy / făncy) blouse and skirt.
8. We plan to stay at the (hōtel / hŏtel) by the beach.
9. How far must we (trāvel / trăvel) to reach the zoo?
10. I think the ice is (sōlid / sŏlid) enough to skate on.

Name: ______________________________ Date: ____________________

Learning About Words That End With a Consonant + "le": *Learning About "Cle" Words*

Many words end with a consonant plus the letters "le." These words are often called the "**Cle**" words.

Examples: tit**le**, eag**le**, nob**le**

Each of the words below is a two-syllable word ending in consonant + le. In each word the consonant + le (Cle) is a separate syllable. The first syllable in some words is open. In other words, the first syllable is closed. Place a macron (¯) or breve (˘) over the vowel in the first syllable to show the long or short vowel sound. Complete the blanks for each word. Write a sentence using each word. The first one has been partially completed for you.

	Word	First Syllable	open/closed	Second Syllable
1.	**title**	tī	open	tle
	Sentence: ______			
2.	**sable**	______	______	______
	Sentence: ______			
3.	**gable**	______	______	______
	Sentence: ______			
4.	**fumble**	______	______	______
	Sentence: ______			
5.	**fable**	______	______	______
	Sentence: ______			
6.	**trifle**	______	______	______
	Sentence: ______			
7.	**stubble**	______	______	______
	Sentence: ______			
8.	**stable**	______	______	______
	Sentence: ______			
9.	**middle**	______	______	______
	Sentence: ______			
10.	**little**	______	______	______
	Sentence: ______			

Name: ______________________________ Date: ____________________

Learning About Words That End With a Consonant + "le": *Finding the Dictionary Spelling for "Cle" Words*

The words below are the dictionary spelling for words that fit the "Cle" spelling pattern. In the column on the right are words that fit the dictionary spelling. Choose the word from the column on the right that matches the dictionary spelling. Write the word for each dictionary spelling on the blank under Word. The first one has been completed for you.

Dictionary Spelling	Word
1. lād′ ′l	ladle
2. kā′ bəl	____________
3. brīd′ ′l	____________
4. fā′ bəl	____________
5. sīd′ ′l	____________
6. trĕs′ əl	____________
7. fĭd′ ′l	____________
8. rin′ kəl	____________
9. tīt′ ′l	____________
10. păd′ ′l	____________
11. hŭd′ ′l	____________
12. ē′ gəl	____________
13. pē′ pəl	____________
14. pŭz′ əl	____________
15. nĭm′ bəl	____________

trestle
fable
title
fiddle
puzzle
paddle
eagle
cable
nimble
ladle
huddle
bridle
wrinkle
people
sidle

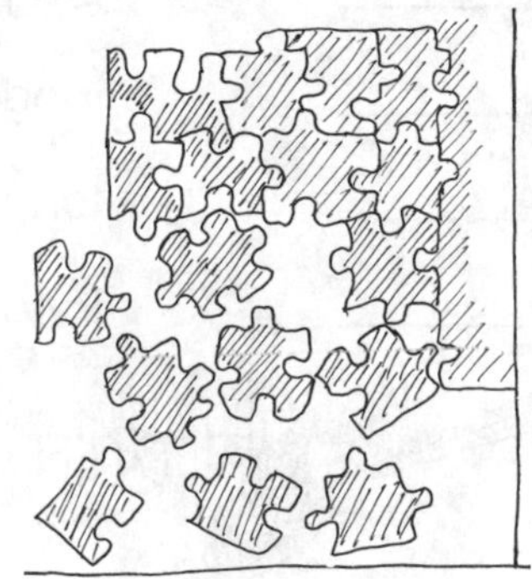

Name: ______________________________ Date: ____________________

Learning About Double Consonants and Syllable Division: *Syllable Division for Words With Double Consonants*

Usually when a word has two consonants between two vowels, the syllable division is between the consonants.

Example: butter = but/ter

Complete the blanks to divide each word into two syllables. Determine the vowel sound for each syllable and circle the correct answer.

	Word	Syllable Division	Vowel Sound First Syllable	Vowel Sound Second Syllable
1.	happen	_______/_______	long / short	long / short / r-contr.
2.	cotton	_______/_______	long / short	long / short / r-contr.
3.	ladder	_______/_______	long / short	long / short / r-contr.
4.	bonnet	_______/_______	long / short	long / short / r-contr.
5.	terror	_______/_______	long / short	long / short / r-contr.
6.	hollow	_______/_______	long / short	long / short / r-contr.
7.	muffin	_______/_______	long / short	long / short / r-contr.
8.	tunnel	_______/_______	long / short	long / short / r-contr.
9.	better	_______/_______	long / short	long / short / r-contr.
10.	picnic	_______/_______	long / short	long / short / r-contr.
11.	batter	_______/_______	long / short	long / short / r-contr.
12.	mutton	_______/_______	long / short	long / short / r-contr.
13.	pillow	_______/_______	long / short	long / short / r-contr.
14.	runner	_______/_______	long / short	long / short / r-contr.
15.	tennis	_______/_______	long / short	long / short / r-contr.

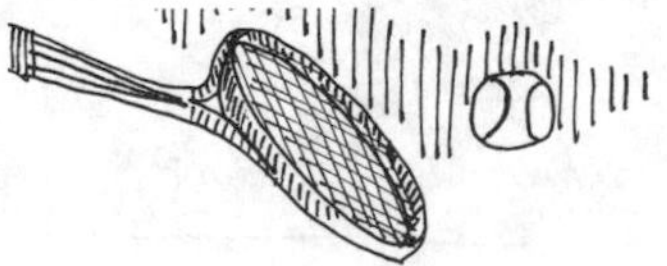

Name: ______________________ Date: ______________

Learning About Double Consonants and Syllable Division: *Syllable Division for Words With Digraphs and Blends*

Usually syllables are not divided between digraphs and blends. Each of the following words has a digraph or blend in a medial position (in the middle of the word). The digraphs are "ph," "th," "sh," and "ch." The blends are "cr," "mp," "st," "nd," "ft," and "nk." Divide each word into two syllables. Do not divide between the blends or digraphs. The first one has been completed for you.

	Digraph	Blend
Example:	tea**ch** / er	se / **cr**et

	Word	Syllable Division	Digraph or Blend	Number of Syllables
1.	teacher	teach / er	ch	2
2.	secret	______ / ______	______	______
3.	weather	______ / ______	______	______
4.	gopher	______ / ______	______	______
5.	siphon	______ / ______	______	______
6.	brother	______ / ______	______	______
7.	preacher	______ / ______	______	______
8.	farther	______ / ______	______	______
9.	jumper	______ / ______	______	______
10.	twister	______ / ______	______	______
11.	winding	______ / ______	______	______
12.	fishing	______ / ______	______	______
13.	lifting	______ / ______	______	______
14.	thinker	______ / ______	______	______
15.	grumpy	______ / ______	______	______

Name: ______________________________ Date: ____________________

Learning About Double Consonants and Syllable Division: *Reviewing Syllable Division*

For each of the following words, place a check on the blank to show the letter pattern that determines the syllable division. If the word has a consonant digraph, blend, or double consonants, write those letters on the blank provided.

	Word	vccv	vcv	digraph/double consonant/blend
1.	button	_____	_____	_______
2.	secret	_____	_____	_______
3.	machine	_____	_____	_______
4.	mother	_____	_____	_______
5.	member	_____	_____	_______
6.	defeat	_____	_____	_______
7.	letter	_____	_____	_______
8.	public	_____	_____	_______
9.	evade	_____	_____	_______
10.	feather	_____	_____	_______
11.	cannon	_____	_____	_______
12.	pilot	_____	_____	_______
13.	cabin	_____	_____	_______
14.	russet	_____	_____	_______
15.	faster	_____	_____	_______
16.	relay	_____	_____	_______
17.	magic	_____	_____	_______
18.	swampy	_____	_____	_______
19.	stutter	_____	_____	_______
20.	conflict	_____	_____	_______

Name: ____________________________ Date: ________________

Learning About Double Consonants and Syllable Division: *Reviewing What Has Been Learned About Syllables*

Each of the words below has two syllables. Read each sentence and choose one of the words below to complete the meaning. Write the word chosen to complete the sentence on the divided blank in each sentence. Write the word as it would be divided into syllables. The first one is completed for you.

final	**father**	**tulip**	**cupid**	**bobbin**
bumper	**spider**	**cement**	**copper**	**comet**
visit	**metal**	**fishing**	**shiver**	**nervous**

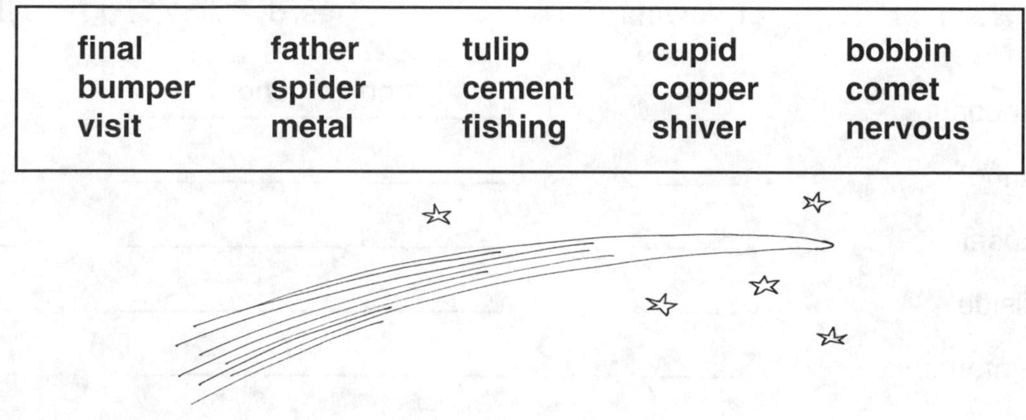

1. The ___com___/___et___ streaked across the heavens with a fiery tail.
2. A beautiful flower, it was first grown in Holland. It is the ________/________.
3. You have one ________/________ chance to improve your test score.
4. The movie was so scary it made me ________/________.
5. ________/________ is often placed on a valentine as a sign of affection.
6. Because she was eager for the game to begin, she was ________/________.
7. When a sidewalk is laid, people often write their names in the wet ________/________.
8. People are like a ________/________; they often weave a web.
9. During spring break, I plan to ________/________ my aunt.
10. In many places of the world, the ________/________ gold is used to adorn temples.
11. When Jack and Jill went ________/________, they caught two trout.
12. Mother's saucepan has a ________/________ bottom.
13. She wound the blue thread on the ________/________.
14. Did you know that my ________/________ works in a factory?
15. The ________/________ on Mrs. Field's car has been dented.

Name: ______________________ Date: ______________

Learning About Double Consonants and Syllable Division: *Compound Words*

Each of the following words is a compound word. Compound words are generally divided into syllables between the root words. Complete the blanks for each word. The first one has been completed for you.

	Compound Word	Number of of Vowels	Vowel Sounds Heard	Number of Syllables
1.	raincoat	4	long a / long o	2
2.	cannot	____	____________	____
3.	sunset	____	____________	____
4.	hillside	____	____________	____
5.	paintbrush	____	____________	____
6.	nobody	____	____________	____
7.	seaweed	____	____________	____
8.	dishpan	____	____________	____
9.	sunlight	____	____________	____
10.	homemade	____	____________	____
11.	bedtime	____	____________	____
12.	upstream	____	____________	____
13.	houseboat	____	____________	____
14.	downtown	____	____________	____
15.	sidewalk	____	____________	____
16.	highway	____	____________	____
17.	fisherman	____	____________	____
18.	overload	____	____________	____
19.	foothold	____	____________	____
20.	icecap	____	____________	____

Name: ______________________________ Date: ________________

Learning About Accented and Unaccented Syllables: *Identifying Accented/Unaccented Syllables*

In words of more than one syllable, you will find accented and unaccented syllables. The **accented syllable** is the syllable with the vowel receiving the greatest emphasis. In the **unaccented syllable**, the vowel sound is like a short "uh" sound. The "uh" sound is much like the sound of short "u." The symbol for the "uh" sound in the unaccented syllable is the schwa (ə).

	Word	Two Syllables	Accented Syllable	Unaccented Syllable
Example:	ticket	tick / et	tick = short "i" sound	et = ə = "uh" sound

Each of the following words is a two-syllable word. Complete the blanks for each word.

	Word	Syllable Division	Accented Syllable	Unaccented Syllable
1.	bacon	______/______	______ = long/short	______ = ___ sound
2.	fatal	______/______	______ = long/short	______ = ___ sound
3.	local	______/______	______ = long/short	______ = ___ sound
4.	letter	______/______	______ = long/short	______ = ___ sound
5.	tunnel	______/______	______ = long/short	______ = ___ sound
6.	pilot	______/______	______ = long/short	______ = ___ sound
7.	final	______/______	______ = long/short	______ = ___ sound
8.	cider	______/______	______ = long/short	______ = ___ sound
9.	robber	______/______	______ = long/short	______ = ___ sound
10.	recent	______/______	______ = long/short	______ = ___ sound
11.	summer	______/______	______ = long/short	______ = ___ sound
12.	cotton	______/______	______ = long/short	______ = ___ sound
13.	motel	______/______	______ = long/short	______ = ___ sound
14.	tiger	______/______	______ = long/short	______ = ___ sound
15.	kitten	______/______	______ = long/short	______ = ___ sound

Name: ______________________________ Date: ____________________

Learning About Accented and Unaccented Syllables: *Identifying the Accented Syllable*

The boldface letters are the accented syllable in each of the following words. Pronounce the word, placing stress on the accented syllable. Complete each sentence using the correctly accented word. Circle the accented syllable on the word you write in each blank.

1. **re** cord re **cord**
   (a) The ________________ shows that he got a good grade.
   (b) You must ________________ the results as each race is finished.
2. **con** tent con **tent**
   (a) The ________________ of the letter was read aloud.
   (b) After lapping up the milk, the cat was ________________.
3. **ob** ject ob **ject**
   (a) The ________________ of the game is to score more points.
   (b) She did not ________________ to the judge's decision.
4. **con** duct con **duct**
   (a) No one could approve of his ________________.
   (b) The police will ________________ a complete review of the case.
5. **reb** el re **bel**
   (a) The sailors chose to ________________ after hearing the captain.
   (b) He often chooses to be a ________________.
6. **con** vict con **vict**
   (a) They have enough evidence to ________________ him.
   (b) Last night a ________________ escaped from jail.
7. **ref** use re **fuse**
   (a) The ________________ will be taken to the dump.
   (b) The man may ________________ to talk.
8. **pro** duce pro **duce**
   (a) He could not ________________ the needed evidence.
   (b) The ________________ will be shipped to the store today.
9. **per** fect per **fect**
   (a) They make a ________________ couple.
   (b) She will ________________ a new of way of writing.
10. **sub** ject sub **ject**
    (a) The ________________ of the sentence is a noun.
    (b) We must not ________________ him to such punishment.

Name: ______________________________ Date: ____________________

Learning About Accented and Unaccented Syllables: *Using the Dictionary to Find the Schwa*

Each of the following words has a syllable with the schwa sound. Use a dictionary and write the dictionary spelling. Complete the blank to indicate if the schwa sound is in the first or second syllable.

Word	Dictionary Phonetic Spelling	Syllable With Schwa Sound
1. alone	____________________	____ first ____ second
2. content	____________________	____ first ____ second
3. object	____________________	____ first ____ second
4. polite	____________________	____ first ____ second
5. contain	____________________	____ first ____ second
6. inland	____________________	____ first ____ second
7. clinker	____________________	____ first ____ second
8. maroon	____________________	____ first ____ second
9. proceed	____________________	____ first ____ second
10. compete	____________________	____ first ____ second
11. compose	____________________	____ first ____ second
12. science	____________________	____ first ____ second
13. hinder	____________________	____ first ____ second
14. wrinkle	____________________	____ first ____ second
15. mobile	____________________	____ first ____ second
16. fever	____________________	____ first ____ second
17. police	____________________	____ first ____ second
18. convey	____________________	____ first ____ second
19. canyon	____________________	____ first ____ second

Name: ______________________________ Date: ____________________

Learning About Accented and Unaccented Syllables: *Learning About Accent in Compound Words*

Each of the following words is a compound word. Use a dictionary and mark the accented and unaccented syllables. Show the accented syllable using the symbol (′).

Compound Word	Syllables
1. hillside	____________________
2. flatboat	____________________
3. layout	____________________
4. icebox	____________________
5. raincoat	____________________
6. baseball	____________________
7. farewell	____________________
8. snowball	____________________
9. forget	____________________
10. weekend	____________________
11. moonlight	____________________
12. downstream	____________________
13. spacecraft	____________________
14. lineman	____________________
15. doghouse	____________________
16. fireplace	____________________
17. inkwell	____________________
18. airplane	____________________
19. nightfall	____________________
20. someone	____________________

Name: ______________________________ Date: ________________

Learning About Affixes and Roots: *Learning to Use the Prefixes “re” and “un”*

Affixes are prefixes and suffixes. **Prefixes** are added to a word before the root wood. **Suffixes** are added after a root word.

Prefix	**Root Word**	**Prefix + Root**
re	pay	repay
Root Word	**Suffix**	**Root + Suffix**
pay	ment	payment

The prefixes “re” and “un” are part of many words. Prefixes change the meaning of the root word. The prefix “un” means “the opposite of” or “not.” The prefix “re” means “again.”

Examples:	**Meaning of Root Word**	**Meaning of Root Word With Prefix**
	happy = feeling good	unhappy = not feeling good
	place = to put	replace = to put again

Add the prefix to the root word to make a new word. Write the new word on the blank. Use the dictionary to find the meaning of the word with the prefix.

	Root Word	**Prefix**	**Prefix + Root**
1.	**safe**	un-	________
	Meaning: ________		
2.	**do**	re-	________
	Meaning: ________		
3.	**pack**	un-	________
	Meaning: ________		
4.	**wind**	un-	________
	Meaning: ________		
5.	**fill**	re-	________
	Meaning: ________		
6.	**open**	re-	________
	Meaning: ________		
7.	**able**	un-	________
	Meaning: ________		
8.	**even**	un-	________
	Meaning: ________		

Name: ______________________ Date: ______________

Learning About Affixes and Roots: *Learning to Use the Prefixes "re" and "un"*

Each of the sentences below has a word with a prefix and root. Circle the word and write the prefix and root on the blanks.

	Prefix	Root
1. He said he would be unable to pay me.	______	________
2. Losing the game made the coach unhappy.	______	________
3. He took the bottle to have it refilled.	______	________
4. Tomorrow the store will reopen.	______	________
5. They were unable to complete the mowing.	______	________
6. The police said he was driving in an unsafe manner.	______	________
7. I asked if I could redo the test.	______	________
8. The team was upset by the uneven playing field.	______	________
9. They must remove the wax.	______	________
10. We must replace the tire.	______	________
11. Can you undo the damage?	______	________
12. I will try to unstick the door.	______	________
13. It is unlikely that she will come to the party.	______	________
14. If you cannot find your paper, you will have to redraw it.	______	________
15. I think that story is untrue.	______	________
16. The puppy went unfed all night.	______	________
17. The new employee was untrained.	______	________
18. Please relabel these boxes.	______	________
19. The losing boxer wanted a rematch.	______	________
20. She is working to reelect the mayor.	______	________

Name: ______________________ Date: ______________

Learning About Affixes and Roots: *Learning to Use the Prefixes "dis" and "im"*

The prefixes "dis" and "im" are found in many words. These prefixes mean "not" or "the opposite of." Combine the prefix "dis" or "im" with the root word to make a new word. Write the word on the blank. Use the root word in a sentence and write the sentence on blank (a). Write a sentence using the root word with the prefix added on blank (b).

Root Word **Root Word With Prefix Added**

1. **obey** ______________
   (a) Sentence (root): ______________________
   (b) Sentence: ______________________
2. **appoint** ______________
   (a) Sentence (root): ______________________
   (b) Sentence: ______________________
3. **polite** ______________
   (a) Sentence (root): ______________________
   (b) Sentence: ______________________
4. **perfect** ______________
   (a) Sentence (root): ______________________
   (b) Sentence: ______________________
5. **arm** ______________
   (a) Sentence (root): ______________________
   (b) Sentence: ______________________
6. **agree** ______________
   (a) Sentence (root): ______________________
   (b) Sentence: ______________________
7. **locate** ______________
   (a) Sentence (root): ______________________
   (b) Sentence: ______________________
8. **proper** ______________
   (a) Sentence (root): ______________________
   (b) Sentence: ______________________

Name: ______________________________ Date: ____________________

Learning About Affixes and Roots: *Finding the Prefix and Root*

Circle the prefix in each of the following words. Write the prefix and root word on the blanks.

Prefixes: re un dis im

	Word	Prefix	Root Word
1.	return	________	________________
2.	recline	________	________________
3.	unclear	________	________________
4.	untie	________	________________
5.	immature	________	________________
6.	impure	________	________________
7.	discover	________	________________
8.	distrust	________	________________

Prefixes can help you tell the meaning of a word. Five very common prefixes are listed below with the meaning of each prefix. Place the prefixes on the blank before the root words to make a new word. Write the meaning of the new word on the blank.

un = not **im** = not **mis** = wrong **sub** = under **anti** = against

1. ________understand: ______________________________
2. ________possible: ______________________________
3. ________certain: ______________________________
4. ________marine: ______________________________
5. ________war: ______________________________
6. ________polite: ______________________________
7. ________spell: ______________________________
8. ________lock: ______________________________
9. ________freeze: ______________________________

Name: ______________________ Date: ______________

Learning About Affixes and Roots: *Learning to Use the Suffixes "ful," "less," and "ly"*

Many words are made from a root with a suffix added.

Example: The root word "**care**" with the suffix "**ful**" becomes a new word: **careful**.

Add the suffix "ful," "less," or "ly" to the root words below to make a new word. Write the suffix on the first blank. Then write the new word on the second blank. Use a dictionary to find the meaning of the word with the suffix. Write a sentence using the word with the suffix.

	Root Word	Suffix	Root + Suffix
1.	**care**	______	____________

Meaning: ______________________________

Sentence: ______________________________

2.	**help**	______	____________

Meaning: ______________________________

Sentence: ______________________________

3.	**hope**	______	____________

Meaning: ______________________________

Sentence: ______________________________

4.	**sad**	______	____________

Meaning: ______________________________

Sentence: ______________________________

5.	**kind**	______	____________

Meaning: ______________________________

Sentence: ______________________________

6.	**man**	______	____________

Meaning: ______________________________

Sentence: ______________________________

Name: ______________________________ Date: ____________________

Learning About Affixes and Roots: *Learning to Use the Suffixes "ful," "less," and "ly"*

Add the suffix "ful," "less," or "ly" to the root words below to make a new word. Write the suffix on the first blank. Then write the new word on the second blank. Use a dictionary to find the meaning of the word with the suffix. Write a sentence using the word with the suffix.

	Root Word	Suffix	Root + Suffix
1.	**pain**	______	____________

Meaning: ____

Sentence: ____

	Root Word	Suffix	Root + Suffix
2.	**play**	______	____________

Meaning: ____

Sentence: ____

	Root Word	Suffix	Root + Suffix
3.	**cheer**	______	____________

Meaning: ____

Sentence: ____

	Root Word	Suffix	Root + Suffix
4.	**use**	______	____________

Meaning: ____

Sentence: ____

	Root Word	Suffix	Root + Suffix
5.	**bad**	______	____________

Meaning: ____

Sentence: ____

	Root Word	Suffix	Root + Suffix
6.	**loud**	______	____________

Meaning: ____

____

Sentence: ________________________

____

Name: ____________________ Date: ______________

Learning About Affixes and Roots: *Using Words With Suffixes*

Read each sentence. Rewrite each of the sentences using the word in bold in your new sentence.

1. They must cross the street with great care. **careful**

   Sentence: ______________________________

2. The kitten was in the mood to play. **playful**

   Sentence: ______________________________

3. The dog's bark was very loud. **loudly**

   Sentence: ______________________________

4. He played with the bunny in a quiet manner. **quietly**

   Sentence: ______________________________

5. She smiles with great cheer. **cheerful**

   Sentence: ______________________________

6. He felt he couldn't get across the street without help. **helpless**

   Sentence: ______________________________

7. The team lost all hope of winning the game. **hopeless**

   Sentence: ______________________________

8. They did not use care when they packed the glass in the box. **careless**

   Sentence: ______________________________

9. She was a kind lady. **kindly**

   Sentence: ______________________________

10. The hammer will be the tool to use to build the birdhouse. **useful**

    Sentence: ______________________________

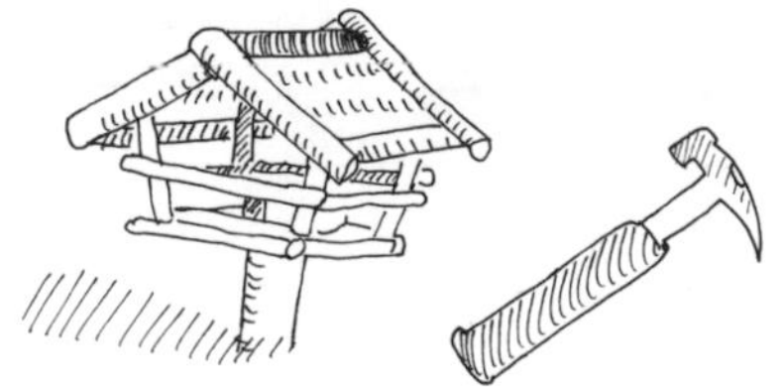

Name: ______________________________ Date: ____________________

Learning About Affixes and Roots: *Learning to Find the Root Word*

When you come to an unknown word, look to see if there are any prefixes or suffixes. Remove the prefixes and suffixes to find the root word. Finding the root word will often help you determine the meaning of the unknown word.

Read each of the following words. Write the prefix, the suffix, and the root word.

	Word	Prefix	Root	Suffix
1.	impoliteness	________	________	________
2.	indirectly	________	________	________
3.	repayment	________	________	________
4.	unhealthful	________	________	________
5.	unarmed	________	________	________
6.	unsuccessful	________	________	________
7.	unbreakable	________	________	________
8.	distrustful	________	________	________
9.	untouched	________	________	________
10.	unreasonable	________	________	________
11.	disrespectful	________	________	________
12.	impassable	________	________	________
13.	misdirected	________	________	________
14.	reassembly	________	________	________
15.	independent	________	________	________
16.	displacement	________	________	________
17.	unfavorable	________	________	________
18.	revisualize	________	________	________
19.	mistaken	________	________	________
20.	immortalize	________	________	________

Name: ______________________________ Date: ____________________

Learning About Affixes and Roots: *Learning to Use Affixes to Pronounce Unknown Words*

When you come to an unknown word with prefixes and/or suffixes, first take off the prefix and/or suffix. Determine the root word. Then determine the vowel sound in the root word. Practice identifying the root word and the vowel sound by completing the following exercise. The first one has been completed for you.

	Word	Prefix	Suffix	Root	Vowel Sound in Root	
1.	unbreakable	un	able	break	long a	short ___
2.	predate	______	______	______	long ___	short ___
3.	profile	______	______	______	long ___	short ___
4.	speechless	______	______	______	long ___	short ___
5.	bemoan	______	______	______	long ___	short ___
6.	faithful	______	______	______	long ___	short ___
7.	painless	______	______	______	long ___	short ___
8.	prepaid	______	______	______	long ___	short ___
9.	dislodge	______	______	______	long ___	short ___
10.	refund	______	______	______	long ___	short ___
11.	trunkful	______	______	______	long ___	short ___
12.	costly	______	______	______	long ___	short ___
13.	refillable	______	______	______	long ___	short ___
14.	homeless	______	______	______	long ___	short ___
15.	hopeless	______	______	______	long ___	short ___
16.	heaviness	______	______	______	long ___	short ___
17.	unflappable	______	______	______	long ___	short ___
18.	frightful	______	______	______	long ___	short ___
19.	priceless	______	______	______	long ___	short ___
20.	biweekly	______	______	______	long ___	short ___

Name: ______________________________ Date: ____________________

Learning About Affixes and Roots: *Reviewing Prefixes, Suffixes, Roots, Inflections, and Compound Words*

Read each word under the column **Word** and complete the blanks that apply to the word.

	Word	Root	Prefix	Suffix	Inflection	Compound Word
1.	rename	______	______	______	______	______ ______
2.	namesake	______	______	______	______	______ ______
3.	playful	______	______	______	______	______ ______
4.	wanted	______	______	______	______	______ ______
5.	overlook	______	______	______	______	______ ______
6.	loyalist	______	______	______	______	______ ______
7.	humorist	______	______	______	______	______ ______
8.	funniest	______	______	______	______	______ ______
9.	girls	______	______	______	______	______ ______
10.	played	______	______	______	______	______ ______
11.	distrustful	______	______	______	______	______ ______
12.	discovered	______	______	______	______	______ ______
13.	somehow	______	______	______	______	______ ______
14.	unforgetful	______	______	______	______	______ ______
15.	unhappiness	______	______	______	______	______ ______
16.	replay	______	______	______	______	______ ______
17.	encampment	______	______	______	______	______ ______
18.	lovable	______	______	______	______	______ ______
19.	subatomic	______	______	______	______	______ ______
20.	download	______	______	______	______	______ ______

Name: ______________________________ Date: ____________________

Learning About Antonyms, Synonyms, and Homonyms: *Learning About Antonyms*

Antonyms are words that have opposite meanings.

Example: **big** and **small** are antonyms; these words are opposite in meaning.

On the right side of the page is a list of words that are antonyms for words in Column I. Write the word on the blank under Column II that means the opposite of the word in Column I.

	Column I	Column II	
1.	hard	________________	**sad**
2.	small	________________	**dull**
3.	hot	________________	**enemy**
4.	noisy	________________	**near**
5.	buy	________________	**remember**
6.	above	________________	**bumpy**
7.	day	________________	**die**
8.	even	________________	**open**
9.	bright	________________	**quiet**
10.	empty	________________	**below**
11.	cry	________________	**sell**
12.	happy	________________	**night**
13.	close	________________	**soft**
14.	far	________________	**cold**
15.	forget	________________	**captive**
16.	complex	________________	**laugh**
17.	live	________________	**full**
18.	free	________________	**large**
19.	friend	________________	**simple**
20.	up	________________	**down**

Name: ______________________ Date: ______________

Learning About Antonyms, Synonyms, and Homonyms:
Learning More About Antonyms

In each of the sentences below is a word in bold. In the word list is a word that means the opposite of the word in bold. Select the word that means the opposite of the bold word and write it on the blank below the bold word.

fake	**export**	**speak**	**weak**	**modern**
major	**wide**	**increase**	**reject**	**dim**

1. In the ruins of the **ancient** village they found many pots for carrying water.

   ____

2. The sale price was a **decrease** from the regular price.

   ____

3. In the **bright** noonday light, sunglasses were needed.

   ____

4. He decided to **choose** a shirt with a blue trim.

   ____

5. The United States **imports** many goods from other nations.

   ____

6. We decided that her problems were **minor**.

   ____

7. The river ran through a very **narrow** gorge.

   ____

8. It was his turn to **listen**.

   ____

9. The coach said weight lifters must be very **strong**.

   ____

10. She always wears **real** diamonds.

    ____

Name: ______________________ Date: ______________

Learning About Antonyms, Synonyms, and Homonyms: *Learning About Synonyms*

Synonyms are words that have the same meaning.

Example: **above** and **over**; These words mean the same thing.

On the right side of the page is a list of words that are synonyms for words in Column I. Write the word on the blank under Column II that means the same as the word in Column I.

	Column I	Column II
1.	bad	____________
2.	dry	____________
3.	beautiful	____________
4.	comic	____________
5.	bend	____________
6.	end	____________
7.	feeble	____________
8.	heal	____________
9.	noisy	____________
10.	leave	____________
11.	strong	____________
12.	wet	____________
13.	simple	____________
14.	wealthy	____________
15.	happy	____________
16.	many	____________
17.	high	____________
18.	flat	____________
19.	safe	____________
20.	cheap	____________

cure
level
protected
powerful
inexpensive
evil
moist
depart
easy
funny
finish
loud
weak
several
arid
rich
cheerful
lovely
curve
lofty

Name: ______________________ Date: ______________

Learning About Antonyms, Synonyms, and Homonyms: *Finding Synonyms*

In each of the sentences below is a word in bold. In the word list is a word that means the same as the word in bold. Select the word that means the same as the bold word and write it on the blank below the bold word.

reduced	**brilliant**	**talk**	**actual**	**powerful**
petty	**thin**	**select**	**sends**	**old**

1. In the ruins of the **ancient** village they found many pots for carrying water.

   ____

2. The sale price had been **decreased** from the regular price.

   ____

3. In the **bright** noonday light sunglasses were needed.

   ____

4. He decided to **choose** a shirt with a blue trim.

   ____

5. The United States **exports** many goods to other nations.

   ____

6. They had a **minor** disagreement.

   ____

7. The river ran like a **narrow** line through the gorge.

   ____

8. It was his turn to **speak**.

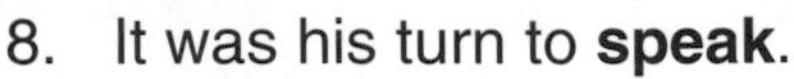

   ____

9. The coach said weight lifters must be very **strong**.

   ____

10. She always wears **real** diamonds.

   ____

Name: ______________________________ Date: ____________________

Learning About Antonyms, Synonyms, and Homonyms: *Learning About Homonyms*

Homonyms are two or more words that have the same pronunciation but are spelled differently and have different meanings.

Example: buy and **by**

The words in the word list below are homonyms for the words in Column I. Write the word on the blank under Column II that is a homonym for the word in Column I. Then use both homonyms in a sentence.

eight	site	week	toe	to	four	their	inn	fair	heel	hour	sole

Column I **Column II**

1. **there** ______________
   Sentence: ______________________________
2. **two** ______________
   Sentence: ______________________________
3. **for** ______________
   Sentence: ______________________________
4. **our** ______________
   Sentence: ______________________________
5. **ate** ______________
   Sentence: ______________________________
6. **tow** ______________
   Sentence: ______________________________
7. **sight** ______________
   Sentence: ______________________________
8. **soul** ______________
   Sentence: ______________________________
9. **weak** ______________
   Sentence: ______________________________
10. **in** ______________
    Sentence: ______________________________

Name: ________________________________ Date: ____________________

Learning About Antonyms, Synonyms, and Homonyms: *Using the Correct Homonyms*

Read each of the following sentences and complete the blank using the correct homonym.

1. **isle** **aisle**
   (a) They walked down the ____________ and sat in the front row.
   (b) They were planning a vacation on a small ____________ in the Atlantic Ocean.
2. **great** **grate**
   (a) The last play of the game was ____________.
   (b) Before lighting the grill, you must clean the ____________.
3. **fair** **fare**
   (a) The ____________ for riding the ferry is twenty-five cents.
   (b) She decided that the teacher had been ____________ when grading the test.
4. **dew** **due**
   (a) The grass was wet from ____________, so we could not mow the lawn.
   (b) I understood the bill was ____________ on the first of each month.
5. **cereal** **serial**
   (a) They always eat ____________ for breakfast.
   (b) To order the new part we will need the ____________ number.

S/N: WTR317984M

CEREAL

6. **foul** **fowl**
   (a) A duck is an example of a ____________.
   (b) She caught the ____________ ball for the third out.
7. **pain** **pane**
   (a) When the ball hit the ____________, it broke.
   (b) He was in great ____________ after falling from the ladder.
8. **sent** **scent**
   (a) Many animals leave a ____________ to mark their territory.
   (b) I ____________ the letter yesterday.
9. **beach** **beech**
   (a) We decided to go to the ____________ for vacation.
   (b) They sat beneath a ____________ tree and finished their homework.
10. **groan** **grown**
    (a) When he read the letter, we heard a loud ____________.
    (b) His father did not have a car until he was ____________.

Glossary of Phonics Terms

Base Word: Often called the root word. Prefixes and suffixes are often added to the base word to make a new word.
base or root = pay
root + prefix = repay
root + suffix = payment

Closed Syllable: A syllable fitting the spelling pattern **consonant-vowel-consonant** (cvc) where the vowel is usually the short sound.
sat pi **lot**

Consonant Blends: The consonant blends are two- or three-letter combinations like "bl," "gl," "st," and "scr." When these letter combinations are found in a word, the sounds of the letters are all heard when pronouncing the word. The consonant blend combinations are usually found at the beginning or end of a word.

Consonant Digraphs: Consonant combinations like "ph," "ch," "gh," "th," "sh," and "ng." When pronounced, these consonant combinations make a sound that is unlike the sounds of the letters that make up the combination.

Consonants: All of the letters of the alphabet except "a," "e," "i," "o," and "u"

Contractions: Words from which one or more letters have been omitted and an apostrophe is used to take the place of the missing letters. **isn't = is not**
there's = there is

Inflections: A letter or letters added at the end of a root word that changes the grammatical function of the word.
's = inflection to indicate possession (boy's)
s = inflection to indicate plural (boys)
ed = inflection to indicate past tense (jumped)
er = inflection to indicate comparison of two things (faster)
est = inflection to indicate comparison of three or more things (fastest)

Long Vowel Sounds: The name of the vowel is the long sound. It is marked with the macron symbol (¯) over the vowel.

Onset: The part of the syllable that comes before the vowel in a word or syllable.
cat = **c** at
The onset is **c** and the rime is **at**.

Open Syllable: A syllable fitting the **consonant-vowel** (cv) spelling pattern where the vowel is usually the long sound.
go **pi** lot

Prefixes: One or more letter combinations added at the beginning of a base word that changes the meaning of the word. **pay** (base word)
re (prefix)
repay (prefix and base word)

Rime: The part of the syllable that comes after the consonant in a word or syllable.
spring = spr **ing**
The onset is **spr** and the rime is **ing**.

Glossary of Phonics Terms

Short Vowel Sounds: The sounds of the vowel in the words **bat**, **bit**, **met**, **pot**, and **nut**. The short sound is marked with the breve (˘) over the vowel.

Suffixes: One or more letter combinations added at the end of a base word that changes the meaning or grammatical function of the word.
pay (base word)
ment (suffix)
payment (base word and suffix)

Syllable: A vowel or vowel and other letters that form a pronounceable unit in a word. A syllable must have a vowel that is heard when the word is pronounced.

The Consonant "c": The consonant "c" has a hard and a soft sound. The soft sound of "c" is the sound in **cent** and **fence**. The hard sound of "c" is the sound in **cat** and **call**.

The Consonant "g": The consonant "g" has a hard and a soft sound. The hard sound of "g" is the sound heard in **go** and **got**. The soft sound of "g" is the sound heard in **gym**.

The Consonant "s": The consonant "s" can have the soft sound heard in **see** or the hard sound heard in **rose**.

Vowel Diphthong: Pairs of vowels like "oi," "oy," and "ou." These vowel pairs make a gliding sound when pronounced.

Vowel-r Combinations: The special sound of the vowels when followed by the letter "r."
far, **fir**, **for**, **fur**, **herd**

Vowels: The letters "a," "e," "i," "o," and "u" and in special situations, the consonants "w" and "y"

"y" as a Consonant or Vowel: The letter "y" is a consonant sound when it is at the beginning of a word or syllable. The letter "y" has the vowel sound of long "a," long "e," or long "i" when it is at the end of a word or syllable.
funny, **day**, **sky**

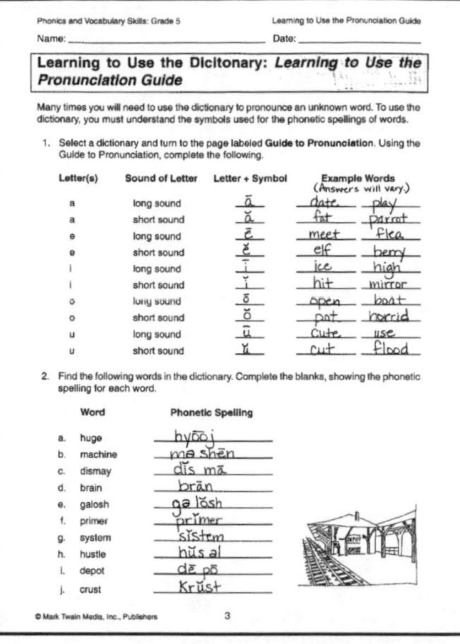

Phonics and Vocabulary Skills: Grade 5 — Learning to Use the Pronunciation Guide

Name: Date:

Learning to Use the Dicitonary: *Learning to Use the Pronunciation Guide*

Many times you will need to use the dictionary to pronounce an unknown word. To use the dictionary, you must understand the symbols used for the phonetic spellings of words.

1. Select a dictionary and turn to the page labeled **Guide to Pronunciation**. Using the Guide to Pronunciation, complete the following.

Letter(s)	Sound of Letter	Letter + Symbol	Example Words (Answers will vary.)	
a	long sound	ā	date	play
a	short sound	ă	fat	parrot
e	long sound	ē	meet	flea
e	short sound	ĕ	elf	berry
i	long sound	ī	ice	high
i	short sound	ĭ	hit	mirror
o	long sound	ō	open	boat
o	short sound	ŏ	pot	horrid
u	long sound	ū	cute	use
u	short sound	ŭ	cut	flood

2. Find the following words in the dictionary. Complete the blanks, showing the phonetic spelling for each word.

	Word	Phonetic Spelling
a.	huge	hyōōj
b.	machine	mə shēn
c.	dismay	dĭs mā
d.	brain	brān
e.	galosh	gə lŏsh
f.	primer	prĭmer
g.	system	sĭstəm
h.	hustle	hŭs əl
i.	depot	dē pō
j.	crust	krŭst

© Mark Twain Media, Inc., Publishers 3

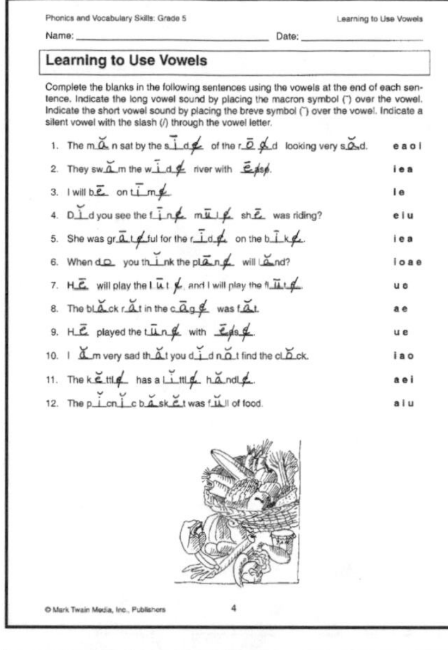

Phonics and Vocabulary Skills: Grade 5 — Learning to Use Vowels

Name: Date:

Learning to Use Vowels

Complete the blanks in the following sentences using the vowels at the end of each sentence. Indicate the long vowel sound by placing the macron symbol (¯) over the vowel. Indicate the short vowel sound by placing the breve symbol (˘) over the vowel. Indicate a silent vowel with the slash (/) through the vowel letter.

1. The măn sat by the sīde of the rōad looking very sŏd. e a o i
2. They swăm the wīde river with Ēase. i e a
3. I will bē on tīme. i e
4. Dĭd you see the tīme mīle shē was riding? e i u
5. She was grātful for the rīde on the bīke. i e a
6. When dō you thĭnk the plāne will lănd? i o a e
7. Hē will play the lūte and I will play the flūte. u e
8. The blăck răt in the cāge was făt. a e
9. Hē played the tūne with ēase. u e
10. I ăm very sad thăt you dĭd nŏt find the clŏck. i a o
11. The kĕttle has a līme hăndle. a e i
12. The pīcnĭc băskĕt was fŭll of food. a i u

© Mark Twain Media, Inc., Publishers 4

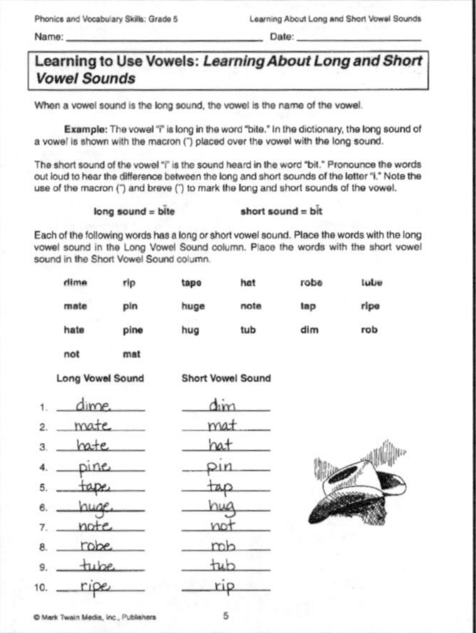

Phonics and Vocabulary Skills: Grade 5 — Learning About Long and Short Vowel Sounds

Name: Date:

Learning to Use Vowels: *Learning About Long and Short Vowel Sounds*

When a vowel sound is the long sound, the vowel is the name of the vowel.

Example: The vowel "i" is long in the word "bite." In the dictionary, the long sound of a vowel is shown with the macron (¯) placed over the vowel with the long sound.

The short sound of the vowel "i" is the sound heard in the word "bit." Pronounce the words out loud to hear the difference between the long and short sounds of the letter "i." Note the use of the macron (¯) and breve (˘) to mark the long and short sounds of the vowel.

long sound = bīte short sound = bĭt

Each of the following words has a long or short vowel sound. Place the words with the long vowel sound in the Long Vowel Sound column. Place the words with the short vowel sound in the Short Vowel Sound column.

dime rip tape hat robe tube mate pin huge note tap ripe hate pine hug tub dim rob not mat

	Long Vowel Sound	Short Vowel Sound
1.	dime	dim
2.	mate	mat
3.	hate	hat
4.	pine	pin
5.	tape	tap
6.	huge	hug
7.	note	not
8.	robe	rob
9.	tube	tub
10.	ripe	rip

© Mark Twain Media, Inc., Publishers 5

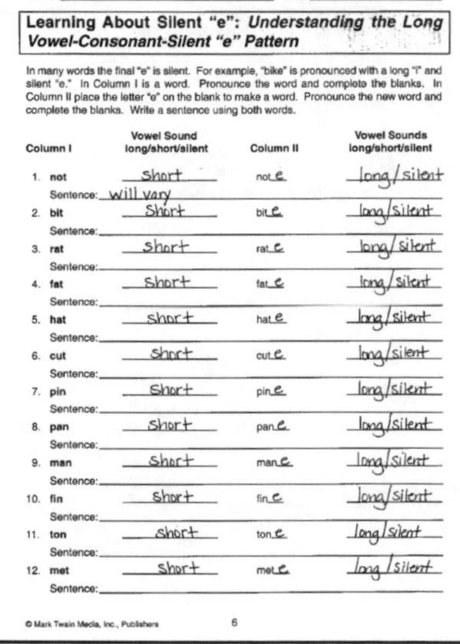

Phonics and Vocabulary Skills: Grade 5 — Understanding the Long Vowel-Consonant-Silent "e" Pattern

Name: Date:

Learning About Silent "e": *Understanding the Long Vowel-Consonant-Silent "e" Pattern*

In many words the final "e" is silent. For example, "bike" is pronounced with a long "i" and silent "e." In Column I is a word. Pronounce the word and complete the blanks. In Column II place the letter "e" on the blank to make a word. Pronounce the new word and complete the blanks. Write a sentence using both words.

Column I	Vowel Sound long/short/silent	Column II	Vowel Sounds long/short/silent
1. not	short	note	long/silent
2. bit	short	bite	long/silent
3. rat	short	rate	long/silent
4. fat	short	fate	long/silent
5. hat	short	hate	long/silent
6. cut	short	cute	long/silent
7. pin	short	pine	long/silent
8. pan	short	pane	long/silent
9. man	short	mane	long/silent
10. fin	short	fine	long/silent
11. ton	short	tone	long/silent
12. met	short	mete	long/silent

Sentence: will vary

© Mark Twain Media, Inc., Publishers 6

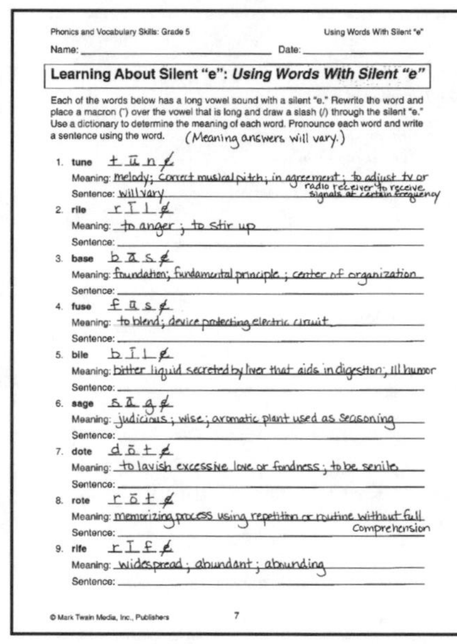

Phonics and Vocabulary Skills: Grade 5 — Using Words With Silent "e"

Name: Date:

Learning About Silent "e": *Using Words With Silent "e"*

Each of the words below has a long vowel sound with a silent "e." Rewrite the word and place a macron (¯) over the vowel that is long and draw a slash (/) through the silent "e." Use a dictionary to determine the meaning of each word. Pronounce each word and write a sentence using the word. (Meaning answers will vary.)

1. tune — t ū n e̸ — Meaning: melody; correct musical pitch; in agreement; to adjust tv or radio receiver to receive signals at certain frequency — Sentence: will vary
2. rile — r ī l e̸ — Meaning: to anger; to stir up
3. base — b ā s e̸ — Meaning: foundation; fundamental principle; center of organization
4. fuse — f ū s e̸ — Meaning: to blend; device protecting electric circuit
5. bile — b ī l e̸ — Meaning: bitter liquid secreted by liver that aids in digestion; ill humor
6. sage — s ā g e̸ — Meaning: judicious; wise; aromatic plant used as seasoning
7. dote — d ō t e̸ — Meaning: to lavish excessive love or fondness; to be senile
8. rote — r ō t e̸ — Meaning: memorizing process using repetition or routine without full comprehension
9. rife — r ī f e̸ — Meaning: widespread; abundant; abounding

© Mark Twain Media, Inc., Publishers 7

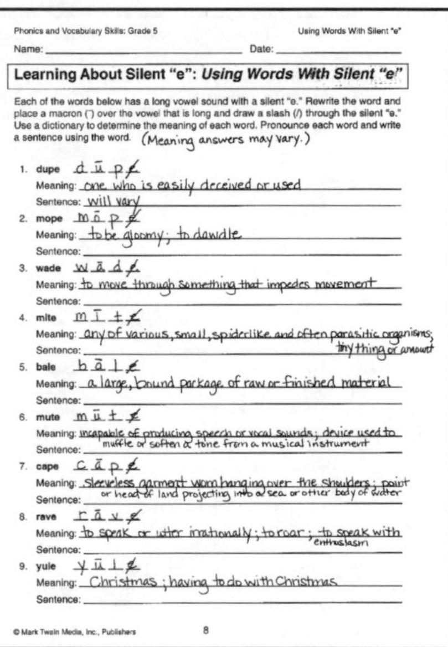

Phonics and Vocabulary Skills: Grade 5 — Using Words With Silent "e"

Name: Date:

Learning About Silent "e": *Using Words With Silent "e"*

Each of the words below has a long vowel sound with a silent "e." Rewrite the word and place a macron (¯) over the vowel that is long and draw a slash (/) through the silent "e." Use a dictionary to determine the meaning of each word. Pronounce each word and write a sentence using the word. (Meaning answers may vary.)

1. dupe — d ū p e̸ — Meaning: one who is easily deceived or used — Sentence: will vary
2. mope — m ō p e̸ — Meaning: to be gloomy; to dawdle
3. wade — w ā d e̸ — Meaning: to move through something that impedes movement
4. mite — m ī t e̸ — Meaning: any of various, small, spiderlike and often parasitic organisms; tiny thing or amount
5. bale — b ā l e̸ — Meaning: a large, bound package of raw or finished material
6. mute — m ū t e̸ — Meaning: incapable of producing speech or vocal sounds; device used to muffle or soften a tone from a musical instrument
7. cape — c ā p e̸ — Meaning: sleeveless garment worn hanging over the shoulders; point or head of land projecting into a sea or other body of water
8. rave — r ā v e̸ — Meaning: to speak or utter irrationally; to roar; to speak with enthusiasm
9. yule — y ū l e̸ — Meaning: Christmas; having to do with Christmas

© Mark Twain Media, Inc., Publishers 8

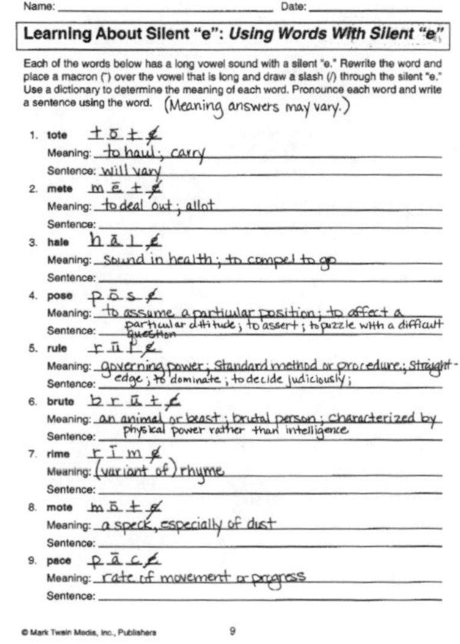

Phonics and Vocabulary Skills: Grade 5 — Using Words With Silent "e"

Name: Date:

Learning About Silent "e": *Using Words With Silent "e"*

Each of the words below has a long vowel sound with a silent "e." Rewrite the word and place a macron (¯) over the vowel that is long and draw a slash (/) through the silent "e." Use a dictionary to determine the meaning of each word. Pronounce each word and write a sentence using the word. (Meaning answers may vary.)

1. tote — t ō t e̸ — Meaning: to haul; carry — Sentence: will vary
2. mete — m ē t e̸ — Meaning: to deal out; allot
3. hale — h ā l e̸ — Meaning: sound in health; to compel to go
4. pose — p ō s e̸ — Meaning: to assume a particular position; to affect a particular attitude; to assert; to puzzle with a difficult question
5. rule — r ū l e̸ — Meaning: governing power; standard method or procedure; straight-edge; to dominate; to decide judiciously
6. brute — b r ū t e̸ — Meaning: an animal or beast; brutal person; characterized by physical power rather than intelligence
7. rime — r ī m e̸ — Meaning: (variant of) rhyme
8. mote — m ō t e̸ — Meaning: a speck, especially of dust
9. pace — p ā c e̸ — Meaning: rate of movement or progress

© Mark Twain Media, Inc., Publishers 9

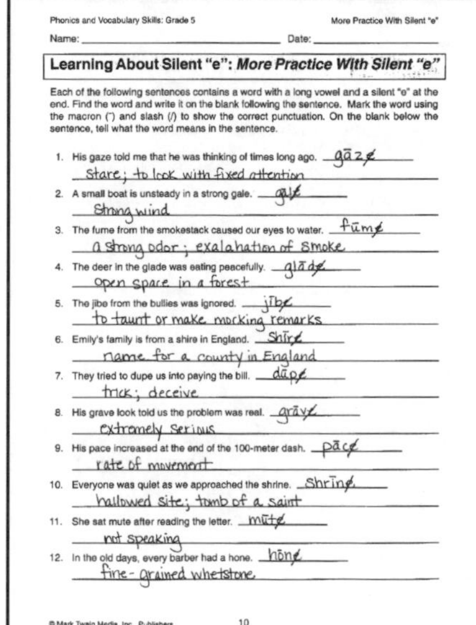

Phonics and Vocabulary Skills: Grade 5 — More Practice With Silent "e"

Name: Date:

Learning About Silent "e": *More Practice With Silent "e"*

Each of the following sentences contains a word with a long vowel and a silent "e" at the end. Find the word and write it on the blank following the sentence. Mark the word using the macron (¯) and slash (/) to show the correct punctuation. On the blank below the sentence, tell what the word means in the sentence.

1. His gaze told me that he was thinking of times long ago. gāze̸ — stare; to look with fixed attention
2. A small boat is unsteady in a strong gale. gāle̸ — strong wind
3. The fume from the smokestack caused our eyes to water. fūme̸ — a strong odor; exalahation of smoke
4. The deer in the glade was eating peacefully. glāde̸ — open space in a forest
5. The jibe from the bullies was ignored. jībe̸ — to taunt or make mocking remarks
6. Emily's family is from a shire in England. shīre̸ — name for a county in England
7. They tried to dupe us into paying the bill. dūpe̸ — trick; deceive
8. His grave look told us the problem was real. grāve̸ — extremely serious
9. His pace increased at the end of the 100-meter dash. pāce̸ — rate of movement
10. Everyone was quiet as we approached the shrine. shrīne̸ — hallowed site; tomb of a saint
11. She sat mute after reading the letter. mūte̸ — not speaking
12. In the old days, every barber had a hone. hōne̸ — fine-grained whetstone

© Mark Twain Media, Inc., Publishers 10

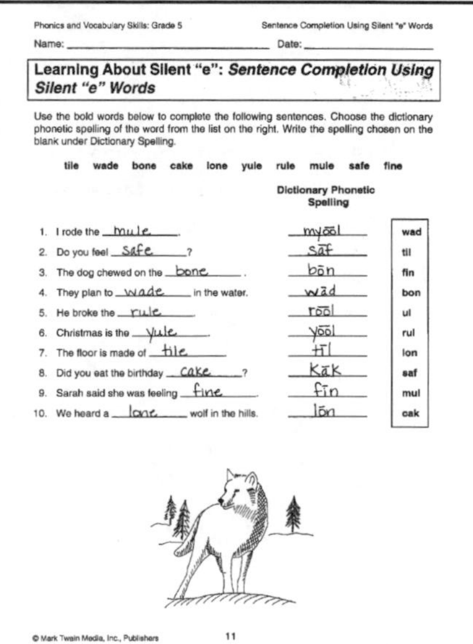

Phonics and Vocabulary Skills: Grade 5 — Sentence Completion Using Silent "e" Words

Name: Date:

Learning About Silent "e": *Sentence Completion Using Silent "e" Words*

Use the bold words below to complete the following sentences. Choose the dictionary phonetic spelling of the word from the list on the right. Write the spelling chosen on the blank under Dictionary Spelling.

tile wade bone cake lone yule rule mule safe fine

	Sentence	Dictionary Phonetic Spelling	
1.	I rode the mule.	myōōl	wad
2.	Do you feel safe?	sāf	til
3.	The dog chewed on the bone.	bōn	fin
4.	They plan to wade in the water.	wād	bon
5.	He broke the rule.	rōōl	ul
6.	Christmas is the yule.	yōōl	rul
7.	The floor is made of tile.	tīl	lon
8.	Did you eat the birthday cake?	kāk	saf
9.	Sarah said she was feeling fine.	fīn	mul
10.	We heard a lone wolf in the hills.	lōn	cak

© Mark Twain Media, Inc., Publishers 11

Phonics and Vocabulary Skills: Grade 5 More Practice Using Silent "e"

Name: ____________ Date: ____________

Learning About Silent "e": *More Practice Using Silent "e"*

Write the correct pronunciation of each of the following words on the dashed lines, placing the macron (¯) over the vowels with the long sound and a slash (/) through silent letters. Write the dictionary spelling of the word on the blank. Then write the meaning of the word on the blank. Finally, use each of the words to make a sentence. (Meaning answers may vary.)

Correct Pronunciation — Dictionary Phonetic Spelling

1. mode — m ō d e̸ — mōd
   Meaning: a manner or method of doing or acting; particular form; current fashion
   Sentence: will vary
2. jute — j ū t e̸ — jüt
   Meaning: fiber of an Asian plant used for sacking and cordage; plant itself
   Sentence:
3. fame — f ā m e̸ — fām
   Meaning: great reputation and recognition; public esteem; renown
   Sentence:
4. hove — h ō v e̸ — hōv
   Meaning: alternate of heave
   Sentence:
5. nape — n ā p e̸ — nāp
   Meaning: back of the neck
   Sentence:
6. ruse — r ū s e̸ — rüz
   Meaning: a trick; artifice; strategem
   Sentence:
7. cage — c ā g e̸ — kāj
   Meaning: a barred or grated enclosure for confining something
   Sentence:
8. rove — r ō v e̸ — rōv
   Meaning: to wander about at random especially over a wide area
   Sentence:
9. mime — m ī m e̸ — mīm
   Meaning: the art of pantomime; a mimic
   Sentence:

© Mark Twain Media, Inc., Publishers 12

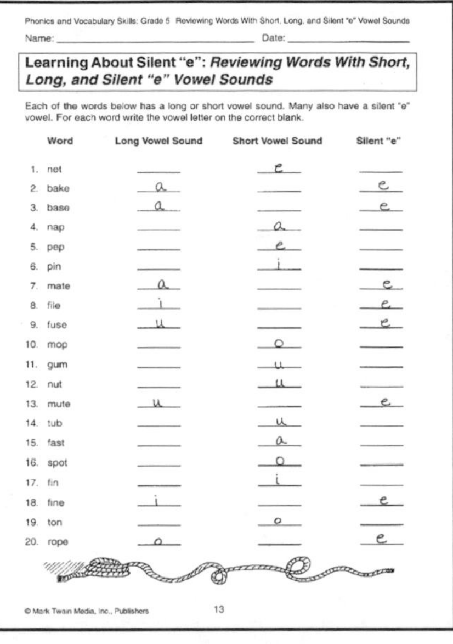

Phonics and Vocabulary Skills: Grade 5 Reviewing Words With Short, Long, and Silent "e" Vowel Sounds

Name: ____________ Date: ____________

Learning About Silent "e": *Reviewing Words With Short, Long, and Silent "e" Vowel Sounds*

Each of the words below has a long or short vowel sound. Many also have a silent "e" vowel. For each word write the vowel letter on the correct blank.

Word	Long Vowel Sound	Short Vowel Sound	Silent "e"
1. net		e	
2. bake	a		e
3. base	a		e
4. nap		a	
5. pep		e	
6. pin		i	
7. mate	a		e
8. file	i		e
9. fuse	u		e
10. mop		o	
11. gum		u	
12. nut		u	
13. mute	u		e
14. tub		u	
15. fast		a	
16. spot		o	
17. fin		i	
18. fine	i		e
19. ton		o	
20. rope	o		e

© Mark Twain Media, Inc., Publishers 13

Phonics and Vocabulary Skills: Grade 5 Learning About the Letter "y" as a Consonant or Vowel

Name: ____________ Date: ____________

Learning About the Letter "y" as a Consonant or Vowel

The letter "y" may be a consonant or a vowel. When the letter begins a word or syllable, the letter has the consonant sound.

Example: y (consonant) - yes be/yond

The letter "y" often has a vowel sound. The vowel sound of "y" may be short "i," long "i," or long "e."

Example: y (vowel) - short "i" (gym); long "i" (by); long "e" (fancy)

In each of the following words "y" has a consonant sound or vowel sound. Write the letter **C** (consonant) or **V** (vowel) on the blank to indicate if "y" has a consonant or vowel sound.

1. C yard 2. V merry 3. V my
4. V cry 5. C yam 6. C yes
7. C yesterday 8. V fly 9. V funny
10. V busy 11. C yew 12. V plenty
13. V try 14. V myself 15. C yearn

In each of the following words the letter "y" makes the short "i," long "i," or long "e" sound. If the "y" makes a short "i" sound, place the word under Column I with a breve (˘). If the "y" makes a long "i" sound, place the word under Column II with a macron (¯). If the "y" makes a long "e" sound, place the word under Column III with a macron (¯).

yap, pony, year, dirty, yell, dye, yarn, cry, yawn, fry, yellow, rye, puppy, penny, you, yolk, heavy, snowy, foggy, sty

Column I (˘)	Column II (¯)	Column III (¯)
yap	cry	puppy
yarn	sty	foggy
year	fry	pony
yawn	dye	penny
you	rye	dirty
yolk		heavy
yell		snowy
yellow		

© Mark Twain Media, Inc., Publishers 14

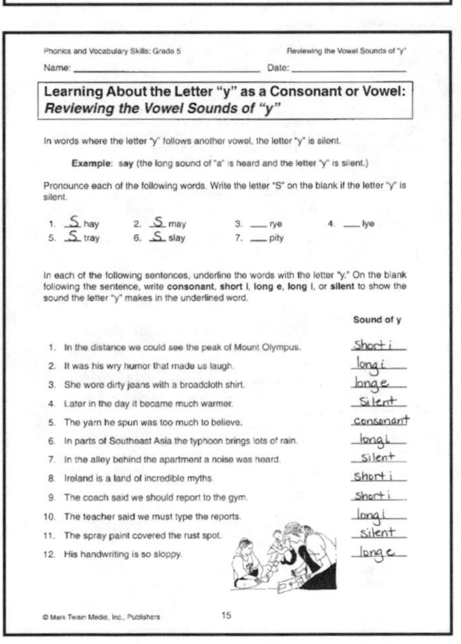

Phonics and Vocabulary Skills: Grade 5 Reviewing the Vowel Sounds of "y"

Name: ____________ Date: ____________

Learning About the Letter "y" as a Consonant or Vowel: *Reviewing the Vowel Sounds of "y"*

In words where the letter "y" follows another vowel, the letter "y" is silent.

Example: say (the long sound of "a" is heard and the letter "y" is silent.)

Pronounce each of the following words. Write the letter "S" on the blank if the letter "y" is silent.

1. S hay 2. S may 3. ___ rye 4. ___ lye
5. S tray 6. S slay 7. ___ pity

In each of the following sentences, underline the words with the letter "y." On the blank following the sentence, write **consonant**, **short** I, **long e**, **long** I, or **silent** to show the sound the letter "y" makes in the underlined word.

	Sound of y
1. In the distance we could see the peak of Mount Olympus.	Short i
2. It was his wry humor that made us laugh.	long i
3. She wore dirty jeans with a broadcloth shirt.	long e
4. Later in the day it became much warmer.	Silent
5. The yarn he spun was too much to believe.	consonant
6. In parts of Southeast Asia the typhoon brings lots of rain.	long i
7. In the alley behind the apartment a noise was heard.	silent
8. Ireland is a land of incredible myths.	Short i
9. The coach said we should report to the gym.	Short i
10. The teacher said we must type the reports.	long i
11. The spray paint covered the rust spot.	silent
12. His handwriting is so sloppy.	long e

© Mark Twain Media, Inc., Publishers 15

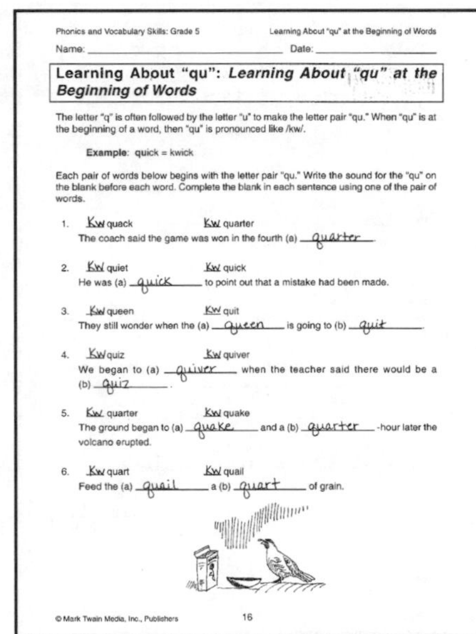

Phonics and Vocabulary Skills: Grade 5 Learning About "qu" at the Beginning of Words

Name: ____________ Date: ____________

Learning About "qu": *Learning About "qu" at the Beginning of Words*

The letter "q" is often followed by the letter "u" to make the letter pair "qu." When "qu" is at the beginning of a word, then "qu" is pronounced like /kw/.

Example: quick = kwick

Each pair of words below begins with the letter pair "qu." Write the sound for the "qu" on the blank before each word. Complete the blank in each sentence using one of the pair of words.

1. Kw quack Kw quarter
   The coach said the game was won in the fourth (a) quarter
2. Kw quiet Kw quick
   He was (a) quick to point out that a mistake had been made.
3. Kw queen Kw quit
   They still wonder when the (a) queen is going to (b) quit
4. Kw quiz Kw quiver
   We began to (a) quiver when the teacher said there would be a (b) quiz
5. Kw quarter Kw quake
   The ground began to (a) quake and a (b) quarter -hour later the volcano erupted.
6. Kw quart Kw quail
   Feed the (a) quail a (b) quart of grain.

© Mark Twain Media, Inc., Publishers 16

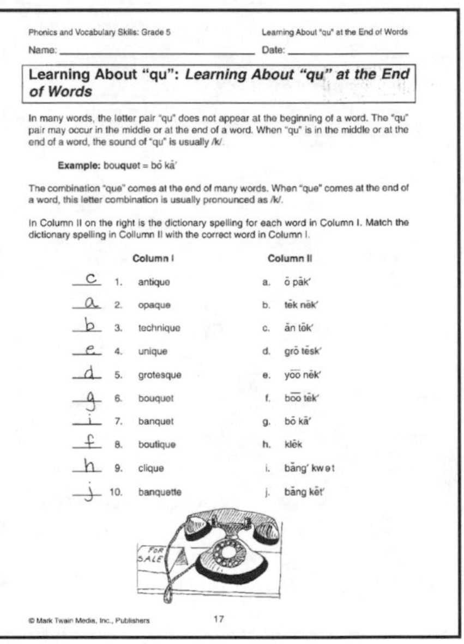

Phonics and Vocabulary Skills: Grade 5 Learning About "qu" at the End of Words

Name: ____________ Date: ____________

Learning About "qu": *Learning About "qu" at the End of Words*

In many words, the letter pair "qu" does not appear at the beginning of a word. The "qu" pair may occur in the middle or at the end of a word. When "qu" is in the middle or at the end of a word, the sound of "qu" is usually /k/.

Example: bouquet = bō kā'

The combination "que" comes at the end of many words. When "que" comes at the end of a word, this letter combination is usually pronounced as /k/.

In Column II on the right is the dictionary spelling for each word in Column I. Match the dictionary spelling in Column II with the correct word in Column I.

	Column I	Column II
c	1. antique	a. ō pāk'
a	2. opaque	b. tek nēk'
b	3. technique	c. ăn tēk'
e	4. unique	d. grō tesk'
d	5. grotesque	e. yōō nēk'
g	6. bouquet	f. bōō tēk'
i	7. banquet	g. bō kā'
f	8. boutique	h. klēk
h	9. clique	i. băng' kwət
j	10. banquette	j. băng kĕt'

© Mark Twain Media, Inc., Publishers 17

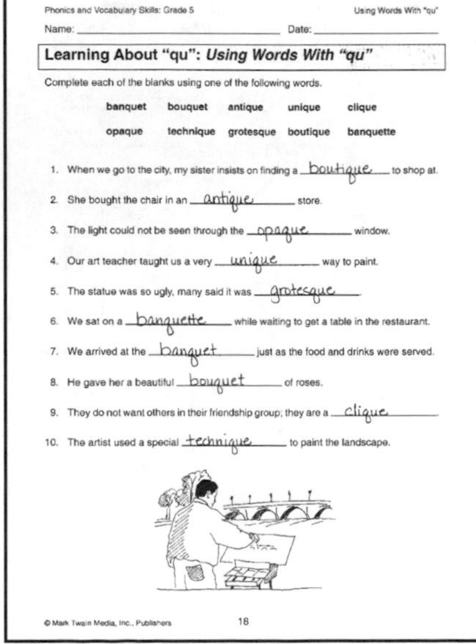

Phonics and Vocabulary Skills: Grade 5 Using Words With "qu"

Name: ____________ Date: ____________

Learning About "qu": *Using Words With "qu"*

Complete each of the blanks using one of the following words.

banquet, bouquet, antique, unique, clique, opaque, technique, grotesque, boutique, banquette

1. When we go to the city, my sister insists on finding a boutique to shop at.
2. She bought the chair in an antique store.
3. The light could not be seen through the opaque window.
4. Our art teacher taught us a very unique way to paint.
5. The statue was so ugly, many said it was grotesque.
6. We sat on a banquette while waiting to get a table in the restaurant.
7. We arrived at the banquet just as the food and drinks were served.
8. He gave her a beautiful bouquet of roses.
9. They do not want others in their friendship group; they are a clique.
10. The artist used a special technique to paint the landscape.

© Mark Twain Media, Inc., Publishers 18

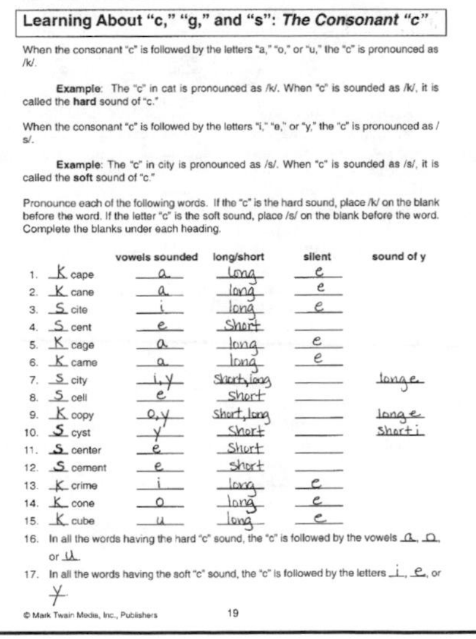

Phonics and Vocabulary Skills: Grade 5 The Consonant "c"

Name: ____________ Date: ____________

Learning About "c," "g," and "s": *The Consonant "c"*

When the consonant "c" is followed by the letters "a," "o," or "u," the "c" is pronounced as /k/.

Example: The "c" in cat is pronounced as /k/. When "c" is sounded as /k/, it is called the **hard** sound of "c."

When the consonant "c" is followed by the letters "i," "e," or "y," the "c" is pronounced as /s/.

Example: The "c" in city is pronounced as /s/. When "c" is sounded as /s/, it is called the **soft** sound of "c."

Pronounce each of the following words. If the "c" is the hard sound, place /k/ on the blank before the word. If the "c" is the soft sound, place /s/ on the blank before the word. Complete the blanks under each heading.

	vowels sounded	long/short	silent	sound of y
1. K cape	a	long	e	
2. K cane	a	long	e	
3. S cite	i	long	e	
4. S cent	e	Short		
5. K cage	a	long	e	
6. K came	a	long	e	
7. S city	i, y	Short, long		long e
8. S cell	e	Short		
9. K copy	o, y	Short, long		long e
10. S cyst	y	Short		short i
11. S center	e	Short		
12. S cement	e	Short		
13. K crime	i	long	e	
14. K cone	o	long	e	
15. K cube	u	long	e	

16. In all the words having the hard "c" sound, the "c" is followed by the vowels a, o, or u.
17. In all the words having the soft "c" sound, the "c" is followed by the letters i, e, or y.

© Mark Twain Media, Inc., Publishers 19

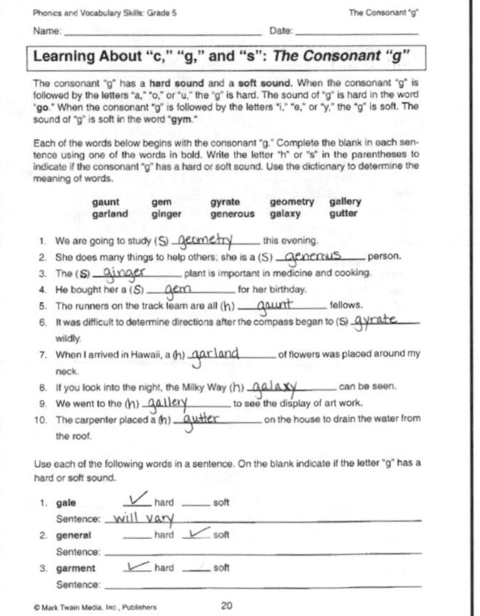

Phonics and Vocabulary Skills: Grade 5 The Consonant "g"

Name: ____________ Date: ____________

Learning About "c," "g," and "s": *The Consonant "g"*

The consonant "g" has a **hard sound** and a **soft sound**. When the consonant "g" is followed by the letters "a," "o," or "u," the "g" is hard. The sound of "g" is hard in the word "**go**." When the consonant "g" is followed by the letters "i," "e," or "y," the "g" is soft. The sound of "g" is soft in the word "**gym**."

Each of the words below begins with the consonant "g." Complete the blank in each sentence using one of the words in bold. Write the letter "h" or "s" in the parentheses to indicate if the consonant "g" has a hard or soft sound. Use the dictionary to determine the meaning of words.

gaunt, gem, gyrate, geometry, gallery, garland, ginger, generous, galaxy, gutter

1. We are going to study (S) geometry this evening.
2. She does many things to help others; she is a (S) generous person.
3. The (S) ginger plant is important in medicine and cooking.
4. He bought her a (S) gem for her birthday.
5. The runners on the track team are all (h) gaunt fellows.
6. It was difficult to determine directions after the compass began to (S) gyrate wildly.
7. When I arrived in Hawaii, a (h) garland of flowers was placed around my neck.
8. If you look into the night, the Milky Way (h) galaxy can be seen.
9. We went to the (h) gallery to see the display of art work.
10. The carpenter placed a (h) gutter on the house to drain the water from the roof.

Use each of the following words in a sentence. On the blank indicate if the letter "g" has a hard or soft sound.

1. **gale** ✓ hard ___ soft
   Sentence: will vary
2. **general** ___ hard ✓ soft
   Sentence:
3. **garment** ✓ hard ___ soft
   Sentence:

© Mark Twain Media, Inc., Publishers 20

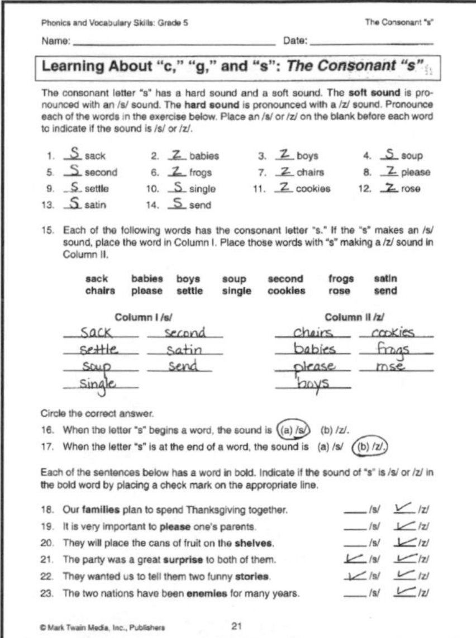
Phonics and Vocabulary Skills: Grade 5 The Consonant "s"

Name: ______ Date: ______

Learning About "c," "g," and "s": *The Consonant "s"*

The consonant letter "s" has a hard sound and a soft sound. The **soft sound** is pronounced with an /s/ sound. The **hard sound** is pronounced with a /z/ sound. Pronounce each of the words in the exercise below. Place an /s/ or /z/ on the blank before each word to indicate if the sound is /s/ or /z/.

1. S sack 2. Z babies 3. Z boys 4. S soup
5. S second 6. Z frogs 7. Z chairs 8. Z please
9. S settle 10. S single 11. Z cookies 12. Z rose
13. S satin 14. S send

15. Each of the following words has the consonant letter "s." If the "s" makes an /s/ sound, place the word in Column I. Place those words with "s" making a /z/ sound in Column II.

sack babies boys soup second frogs satin chairs please settle single cookies rose send

Column I /s/		Column II /z/	
sack	second	chairs	cookies
settle	satin	babies	frogs
soup	send	please	rose
single		boys	

Circle the correct answer.

16. When the letter "s" begins a word, the sound is **(a) /s/** (b) /z/.
17. When the letter "s" is at the end of a word, the sound is (a) /s/ **(b) /z/.**

Each of the sentences below has a word in bold. Indicate if the sound of "s" is /s/ or /z/ in the bold word by placing a check mark on the appropriate line.

18. Our **families** plan to spend Thanksgiving together. ___ /s/ ✓ /z/
19. It is very important to **please** one's parents. ___ /s/ ✓ /z/
20. They will place the cans of fruit on the **shelves**. ___ /s/ ✓ /z/
21. The party was a great **surprise** to both of them. ✓ /s/ ✓ /z/
22. They wanted us to tell them two funny **stories**. ✓ /s/ ✓ /z/
23. The two nations have been **enemies** for many years. ___ /s/ ✓ /z/

© Mark Twain Media, Inc., Publishers 21

Phonics and Vocabulary Skills: Grade 5 Understanding Phonetic Spelling

Name: ______ Date: ______

Learning About "c," "g," and "s": *Understanding Phonetic Spelling*

When using the dictionary, the phonetic spelling of a word helps you pronounce the word. Column I on the right lists the dictionary phonetic spelling of common words that contain the sounds of "c," "g," and "s." Write the correct spelling of the word on the blank in Column II.

	Column I	Column II	Definition
1.	kăn′ dē	candy	good to eat
2.	gĕst	guest	recipient of hospitality
3.	kăn′ səl	cancel	draw lines across
4.	sīt	cite	mention specifically
5.	glâr	glare	dazzling light
6.	jī′ rō	gyro	a ring or circle
7.	sĭv′ əl	civil	refers to the state and its laws
8.	jĕl′ ə tĭn	gelatin	jellylike
9.	glĭmps	glimpse	quick look or glance
10.	sĭnch	cinch	something sure to be accomplished
11.	sī′ klōn	cyclone	a storm of great destruction
12.	krōō sād′	crusade	to support a cause
13.	găj′ ĭt	gadget	small mechanical device
14.	gā′ lē	gaily	merrily
15.	kăn′ dĭd	candid	outspoken, frank
16.	jĭp	gyp	cheat or swindle
17.	kōm	comb	used to groom hair
18.	gōst	ghost	a spirit
19.	sĭm′ bəl	cymbal	musical instrument
20.	glīd	glide	move with smooth easy motion

© Mark Twain Media, Inc., Publishers 22

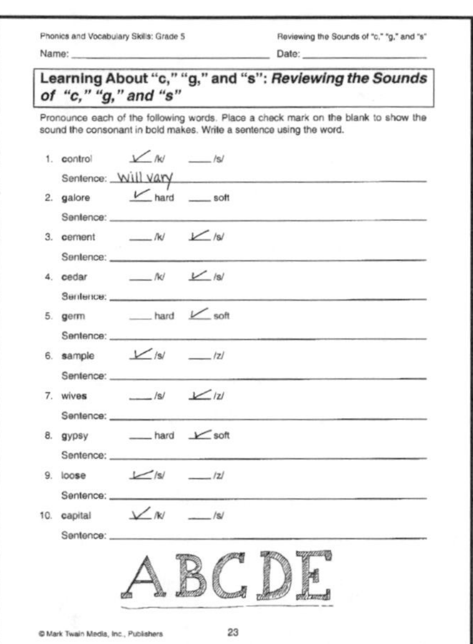
Phonics and Vocabulary Skills: Grade 5 Reviewing the Sounds of "c," "g," and "s"

Name: ______ Date: ______

Learning About "c," "g," and "s": *Reviewing the Sounds of "c," "g," and "s"*

Pronounce each of the following words. Place a check mark on the blank to show the sound the consonant in bold makes. Write a sentence using the word.

1. **c**ontrol ✓ /k/ ___ /s/
Sentence: will vary
2. **g**alore ✓ hard ___ soft
Sentence: ______
3. **c**ement ___ /k/ ✓ /s/
Sentence: ______
4. **c**edar ___ /k/ ✓ /s/
Sentence: ______
5. **g**erm ___ hard ✓ soft
Sentence: ______
6. **s**ample ✓ /s/ ___ /z/
Sentence: ______
7. wive**s** ___ /s/ ✓ /z/
Sentence: ______
8. **g**ypsy ___ hard ✓ soft
Sentence: ______
9. loo**s**e ✓ /s/ ___ /z/
Sentence: ______
10. **c**apital ✓ /k/ ___ /s/
Sentence: ______

ABCDE

© Mark Twain Media, Inc., Publishers 23

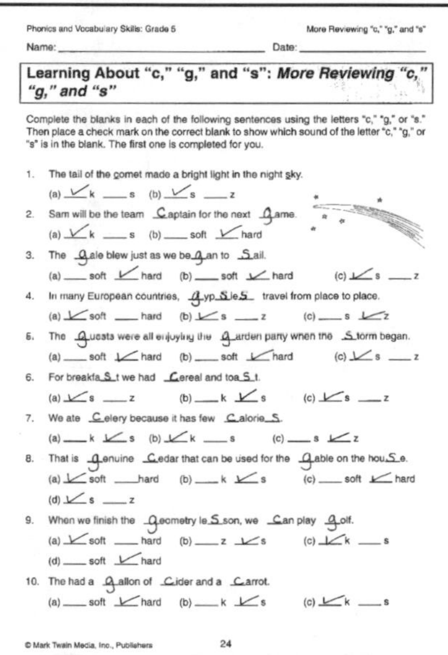
Phonics and Vocabulary Skills: Grade 5 More Reviewing "c," "g," and "s"

Name: ______ Date: ______

Learning About "c," "g," and "s": *More Reviewing "c," "g," and "s"*

Complete the blanks in each of the following sentences using the letters "c," "g," or "s." Then place a check mark on the correct blank to show which sound of the letter "c," "g," or "s" is in the blank. The first one is completed for you.

1. The tail of the comet made a bright light in the night sky.
(a) ✓ k ___ s (b) ✓ s ___ z
2. Sam will be the team Captain for the next game.
(a) ✓ k ___ s (b) ___ soft ✓ hard
3. The gale blew just as we began to Sail.
(a) ___ soft ✓ hard (b) ___ soft ✓ hard (c) ✓ s ___ z
4. In many European countries, gypSieS travel from place to place.
(a) ✓ soft ___ hard (b) ✓ s ___ z (c) ___ s ✓ z
5. The guests were all enjoying the garden party when the Storm began.
(a) ___ soft ✓ hard (b) ___ soft ✓ hard (c) ✓ s ___ z
6. For breakfaSt we had Cereal and toaSt.
(a) ✓ s ___ z (b) ___ k ✓ s (c) ✓ s ___ z
7. We ate Celery because it has few CalorieS.
(a) ___ k ✓ s (b) ✓ k ___ s (c) ___ s ✓ z
8. That is genuine Cedar that can be used for the gable on the houSe.
(a) ✓ soft ___ hard (b) ___ k ✓ s (c) ___ soft ✓ hard
(d) ✓ s ___ z
9. When we finish the geometry leSson, we Can play golf.
(a) ✓ soft ___ hard (b) ___ z ✓ s (c) ✓ k ___ s
(d) ___ soft ✓ hard
10. The had a gallon of Cider and a Carrot.
(a) ___ soft ✓ hard (b) ___ k ✓ s (c) ✓ k ___ s

© Mark Twain Media, Inc., Publishers 24

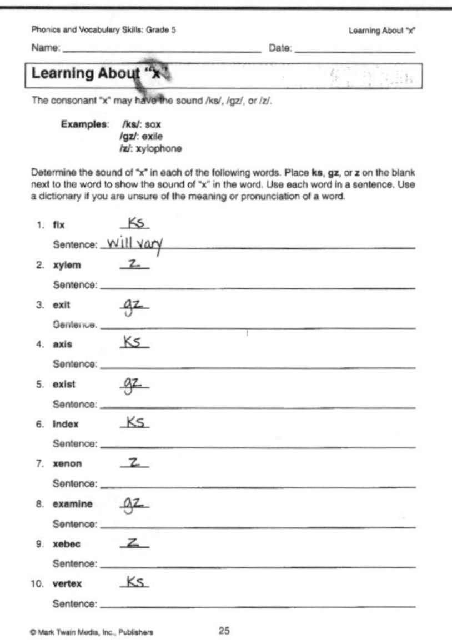
Phonics and Vocabulary Skills: Grade 5 Learning About "x"

Name: ______ Date: ______

Learning About "x"

The consonant "x" may have the sound /ks/, /gz/, or /z/.

Examples: ***/ks/***: sox
/gz/: exile
/z/: xylophone

Determine the sound of "x" in each of the following words. Place **ks**, **gz**, or **z** on the blank next to the word to show the sound of "x" in the word. Use each word in a sentence. Use a dictionary if you are unsure of the meaning or pronunciation of a word.

1. **fix** Ks
Sentence: will vary
2. **xylem** z
Sentence: ______
3. **exit** gz
Sentence: ______
4. **axis** Ks
Sentence: ______
5. **exist** gz
Sentence: ______
6. **index** Ks
Sentence: ______
7. **xenon** z
Sentence: ______
8. **examine** gz
Sentence: ______
9. **xebec** z
Sentence: ______
10. **vertex** Ks
Sentence: ______

© Mark Twain Media, Inc., Publishers 25

Phonics and Vocabulary Skills: Grade 5 Making Words Using Beginning Consonant Blends

Name: ______ Date: ______

Learning About Consonant Blends: *Making Words Using Beginning Consonant Blends*

Consonant blends are two- or three-letter consonants that are blended together when sounded in a word.

Examples: blind = **bl**ind trust = **tr**ust

Use the following blends and make new words that match the meanings. Then write the word on the blank using the macron (¯) to show the long vowel sound and a slash (/) to show the silent "e" for each word. Write the new word in a sentence that matches the meaning.

fl bl gr gl br fr sl cl dr pl pr

1. g l ide glīd⁄e meaning: slip over a smooth surface
Sentence: will vary
2. g r ave grāv⁄e meaning: burial site
Sentence: ______
3. g r aze grāz⁄e meaning: brush lightly in passing
Sentence: ______
4. f l ute flūt⁄e meaning: musical instrument
Sentence: ______
5. c l ose clōs⁄e meaning: finish or conclude
Sentence: ______
6. c l ue clū⁄e meaning: a hint
Sentence: ______
7. g r ape grāp⁄e meaning: fruit used to make jelly
Sentence: ______
8. f l are flār⁄e meaning: blazing light used as a signal
Sentence: ______
9. b l ame blām⁄e meaning: to hold responsible for error
Sentence: ______
10. g l ade glād⁄e meaning: clear space in a forest
Sentence: ______
11. g r ipe grīp⁄e meaning: to complain
Sentence: ______
12. p r obe prōb⁄e meaning: to search or explore
Sentence: ______

© Mark Twain Media, Inc., Publishers 26

Phonics and Vocabulary Skills: Grade 5 More Work With Blends

Name: ______ Date: ______

Learning About Consonant Blends: *More Work With Blends*

Replace the blends in the words in the column under **Word** with one of the blends below to make a new word. Choose a blend to make a new word that rhymes. Show the correct markings for long vowel sounds and silent letters. Use the new word in a sentence.

dr bl sm pr tr sl gr spl gl

Answers may vary.

Word	New Word	New Word With Markings for Vowel Sound and Silent Letters
1. **slate**	g r ate	grāt⁄e
Sentence: will vary		
2. **slope**	g r ope	grōp⁄e
Sentence:		
3. **trade**	b l ade	blād⁄e
Sentence:		
4. **crime**	g r ime	grīm⁄e
Sentence:		
5. **slice**	s p l ice	splīc⁄e
Sentence:		
6. **frame**	b l ame	blām⁄e
Sentence:		
7. **clove**	g r ove	grōv⁄e
Sentence:		
8. **craze**	g l aze	glāz⁄e
Sentence:		
9. **bloke**	s m oke	smōk⁄e
Sentence:		
10. **flake**	d r ake	drāk⁄e
Sentence:		

© Mark Twain Media, Inc., Publishers 27

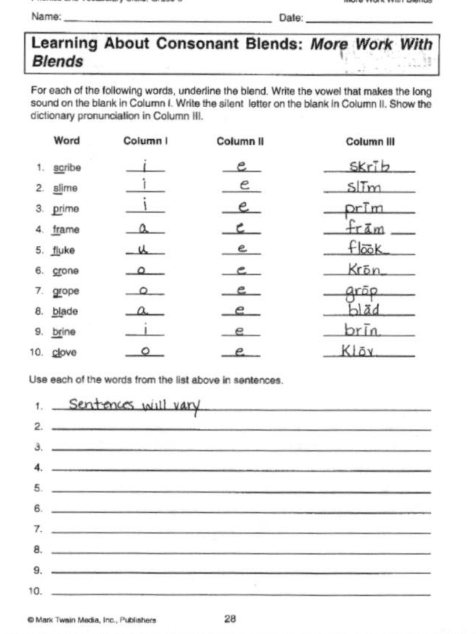
Phonics and Vocabulary Skills: Grade 5 More Work With Blends

Name: ______ Date: ______

Learning About Consonant Blends: *More Work With Blends*

For each of the following words, underline the blend. Write the vowel that makes the long sound on the blank in Column I. Write the silent letter on the blank in Column II. Show the dictionary pronunciation in Column III.

Word	Column I	Column II	Column III
1. scribe	i	e	skrīb
2. slime	i	e	slīm
3. prime	i	e	prīm
4. frame	a	e	frām
5. fluke	u	e	flōōk
6. crone	o	e	Krōn
7. grope	o	e	grōp
8. blade	a	e	blād
9. brine	i	e	brīn
10. clove	o	e	Klōv

Use each of the words from the list above in sentences.

1. Sentences will vary
2. ______
3. ______
4. ______
5. ______
6. ______
7. ______
8. ______
9. ______
10. ______

© Mark Twain Media, Inc., Publishers 28

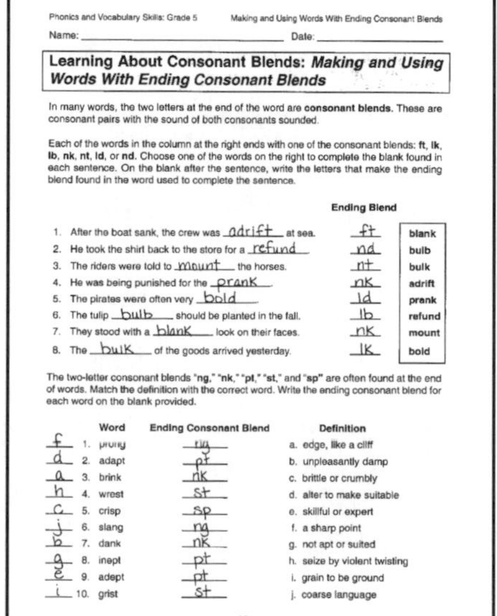
Phonics and Vocabulary Skills: Grade 5 Making and Using Words With Ending Consonant Blends

Name: ______ Date: ______

Learning About Consonant Blends: *Making and Using Words With Ending Consonant Blends*

In many words, the two letters at the end of the word are **consonant blends.** These are consonant pairs with the sound of both consonants sounded.

Each of the words in the column at the right ends with one of the consonant blends: **ft**, **lk**, **lb**, **nk**, **nt**, **ld**, or **nd.** Choose one of the words on the right to complete the blank found in each sentence. On the blank after the sentence, write the letters that make the ending blend found in the word used to complete the sentence.

	Ending Blend	
1. After the boat sank, the crew was adrift at sea.	ft	**blank**
2. He took the shirt back to the store for a refund.	nd	**bulb**
3. The riders were told to mount the horses.	nt	**bulk**
4. He was being punished for the prank.	nk	**adrift**
5. The pirates were often very bold.	ld	**prank**
6. The tulip bulb should be planted in the fall.	lb	**refund**
7. They stood with a blank look on their faces.	nk	**mount**
8. The bulk of the goods arrived yesterday.	lk	**bold**

The two-letter consonant blends "**ng**," "**nk**," "**pt**," "**st**," and "**sp**" are often found at the end of words. Match the definition with the correct word. Write the ending consonant blend for each word on the blank provided.

	Word	Ending Consonant Blend	Definition
f	1. prong	ng	a. edge, like a cliff
d	2. adapt	pt	b. unpleasantly damp
a	3. brink	nk	c. brittle or crumbly
h	4. wrest	st	d. alter to make suitable
c	5. crisp	sp	e. skillful or expert
j	6. slang	ng	f. a sharp point
b	7. dank	nk	g. not apt or suited
g	8. inept	pt	h. seize by violent twisting
e	9. adept	pt	i. grain to be ground
i	10. grist	st	j. coarse language

© Mark Twain Media, Inc., Publishers 29

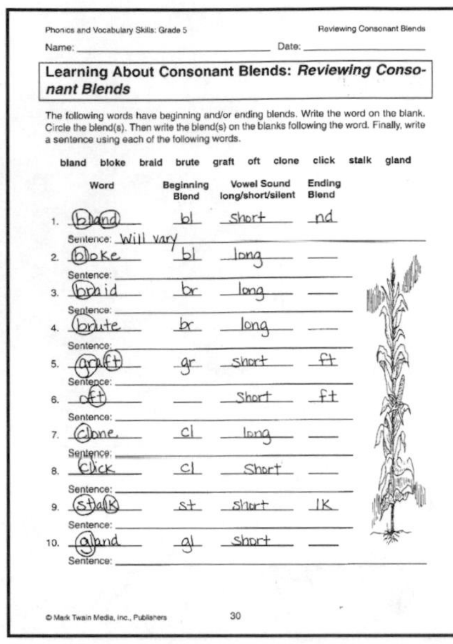

Phonics and Vocabulary Skills: Grade 5 — Reviewing Consonant Blends

Name: ______ Date: ______

Learning About Consonant Blends: *Reviewing Consonant Blends*

The following words have beginning and/or ending blends. Write the word on the blank. Circle the blend(s). Then write the blend(s) on the blanks following the word. Finally, write a sentence using each of the following words.

bland bloke braid brute graft oft clone click stalk gland

	Word	Beginning Blend	Vowel Sound long/short/silent	Ending Blend
1.	bland	bl	short	nd
2.	bloke	bl	long	
3.	braid	br	long	
4.	brute	br	long	
5.	graft	gr	short	ft
6.	oft		Short	ft
7.	clone	cl	long	
8.	click	cl	Short	
9.	stalk	st	short	lK
10.	gland	gl	short	

Sentence: Will vary

© Mark Twain Media, Inc., Publishers 30

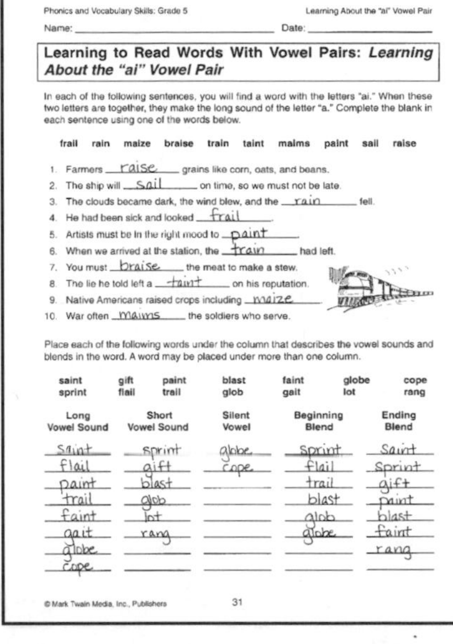

Phonics and Vocabulary Skills: Grade 5 — Learning About the "ai" Vowel Pair

Name: ______ Date: ______

Learning to Read Words With Vowel Pairs: *Learning About the "ai" Vowel Pair*

In each of the following sentences, you will find a word with the letters "ai." When these two letters are together, they make the long sound of the letter "a." Complete the blank in each sentence using one of the words below.

frail rain maize braise train taint maims paint sail raise

1. Farmers raise grains like corn, oats, and beans.
2. The ship will sail on time, so we must not be late.
3. The clouds became dark, the wind blew, and the rain fell.
4. He had been sick and looked frail.
5. Artists must be in the right mood to paint.
6. When we arrived at the station, the train had left.
7. You must braise the meat to make a stew.
8. The lie he told left a taint on his reputation.
9. Native Americans raised crops including maize.
10. War often maims the soldiers who serve.

Place each of the following words under the column that describes the vowel sounds and blends in the word. A word may be placed under more than one column.

saint gift paint blast faint globe cope sprint flail trail glob gait lot rang

Long Vowel Sound	Short Vowel Sound	Silent Vowel	Beginning Blend	Ending Blend
saint	sprint	globe	sprint	Saint
flail	gift	cope	flail	Sprint
paint	blast		trail	gift
trail	glob		blast	paint
faint	lot		glob	blast
gait	rang		globe	faint
globe				rang
cope				

© Mark Twain Media, Inc., Publishers 31

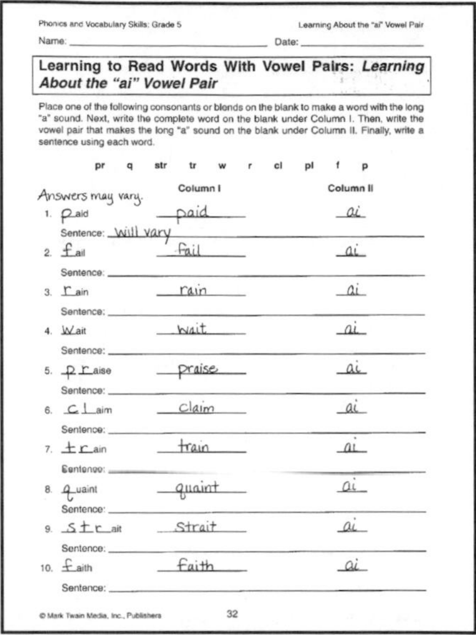

Phonics and Vocabulary Skills: Grade 5 — Learning About the "ai" Vowel Pair

Name: ______ Date: ______

Learning to Read Words With Vowel Pairs: *Learning About the "ai" Vowel Pair*

Place one of the following consonants or blends on the blank to make a word with the long "a" sound. Next, write the complete word on the blank under Column I. Then, write the vowel pair that makes the long "a" sound on the blank under Column II. Finally, write a sentence using each word.

pr q str tr w r cl pl f p

Answers may vary.

		Column I	Column II
1.	p aid	paid	ai
2.	f ail	fail	ai
3.	r ain	rain	ai
4.	w ait	wait	ai
5.	p r aise	praise	ai
6.	c l aim	claim	ai
7.	t r ain	train	ai
8.	q uaint	quaint	ai
9.	s t r ait	strait	ai
10.	f aith	faith	ai

Sentence: Will vary

© Mark Twain Media, Inc., Publishers 32

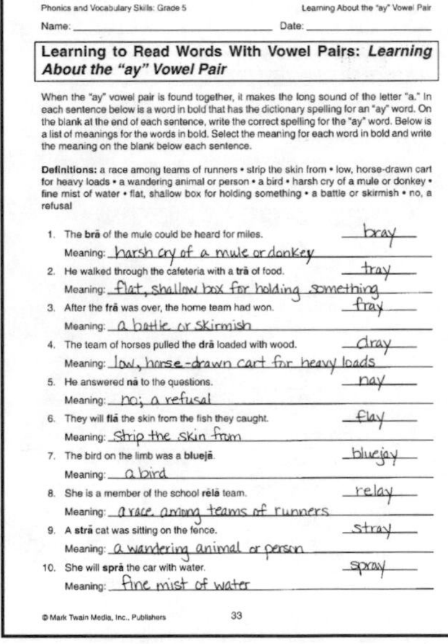

Phonics and Vocabulary Skills: Grade 5 — Learning About the "ay" Vowel Pair

Name: ______ Date: ______

Learning to Read Words With Vowel Pairs: *Learning About the "ay" Vowel Pair*

When the "ay" vowel pair is found together, it makes the long sound of the letter "a." In each sentence below is a word in bold that has the dictionary spelling for an "ay" word. On the blank at the end of each sentence, write the correct spelling for the "ay" word. Below is a list of meanings for the words in bold. Select the meaning for each word in bold and write the meaning on the blank below each sentence.

Definitions: a race among teams of runners • strip the skin from • low, horse-drawn cart for heavy loads • a wandering animal or person • a bird • harsh cry of a mule or donkey • fine mist of water • flat, shallow box for holding something • a battle or skirmish • no, a refusal

1. The **brā** of the mule could be heard for miles. bray
   Meaning: harsh cry of a mule or donkey
2. He walked through the cafeteria with a **trā** of food. tray
   Meaning: flat, shallow box for holding something
3. After the **frā** was over, the home team had won. fray
   Meaning: a battle or skirmish
4. The team of horses pulled the **drā** loaded with wood. dray
   Meaning: low, horse-drawn cart for heavy loads
5. He answered **nā** to the questions. nay
   Meaning: no; a refusal
6. They will **flā** the skin from the fish they caught. flay
   Meaning: strip the skin from
7. The bird on the limb was a **bluejā**. bluejay
   Meaning: a bird
8. She is a member of the school **rēlā** team. relay
   Meaning: a race among teams of runners
9. A **strā** cat was sitting on the fence. stray
   Meaning: a wandering animal or person
10. She will **sprā** the car with water. spray
   Meaning: fine mist of water

© Mark Twain Media, Inc., Publishers 33

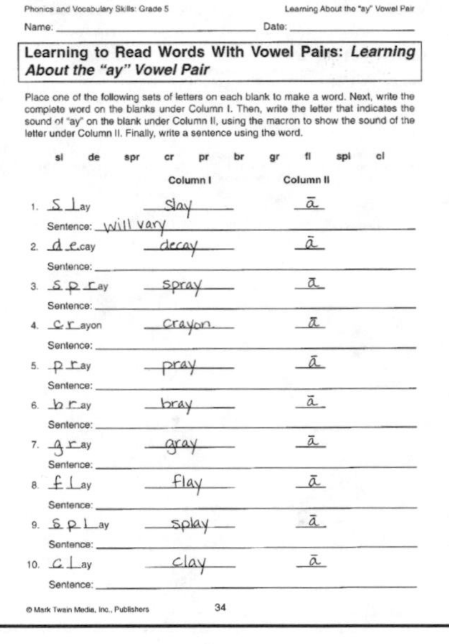

Phonics and Vocabulary Skills: Grade 5 — Learning About the "ay" Vowel Pair

Name: ______ Date: ______

Learning to Read Words With Vowel Pairs: *Learning About the "ay" Vowel Pair*

Place one of the following sets of letters on each blank to make a word. Next, write the complete word on the blanks under Column I. Then, write the letter that indicates the sound of "ay" on the blank under Column II, using the macron to show the sound of the letter under Column II. Finally, write a sentence using the word.

sl de spr cr pr br gr fl spl cl

		Column I	Column II
1.	s l ay	slay	ā
2.	d e cay	decay	ā
3.	s p r ay	spray	ā
4.	c r ayon	crayon	ā
5.	p r ay	pray	ā
6.	b r ay	bray	ā
7.	g r ay	gray	ā
8.	f l ay	flay	ā
9.	s p l ay	splay	ā
10.	c l ay	clay	ā

Sentence: will vary

© Mark Twain Media, Inc., Publishers 34

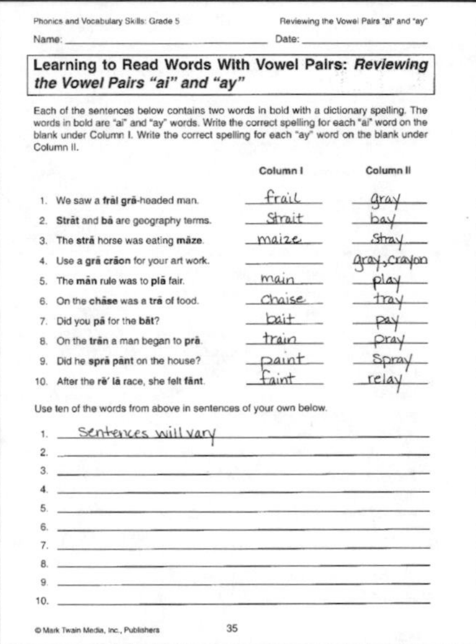

Phonics and Vocabulary Skills: Grade 5 — Reviewing the Vowel Pairs "ai" and "ay"

Name: ______ Date: ______

Learning to Read Words With Vowel Pairs: *Reviewing the Vowel Pairs "ai" and "ay"*

Each of the sentences below contains two words in bold with a dictionary spelling. The words in bold are "ai" and "ay" words. Write the correct spelling for each "ai" word on the blank under Column I. Write the correct spelling for each "ay" word on the blank under Column II.

		Column I	Column II
1.	We saw a **frāl grā**-headed man.	frail	gray
2.	**Strāt** and **bā** are geography terms.	Strait	bay
3.	The **strā** horse was eating **māze**.	maize	Stray
4.	Use a **grā crāon** for your art work.		gray, crayon
5.	The **mān** rule was to **plā** fair.	main	play
6.	On the **chāse** was a **trā** of food.	chaise	tray
7.	Did you **pā** for the **bāt**?	bait	pay
8.	On the **trān** a man began to **prā**.	train	pray
9.	Did he **sprā pānt** on the house?	paint	Spray
10.	After the **rē' lā** race, she felt **fānt**.	faint	relay

Use ten of the words from above in sentences of your own below.

1. Sentences will vary
2.
3.
4.
5.
6.
7.
8.
9.
10.

© Mark Twain Media, Inc., Publishers 35

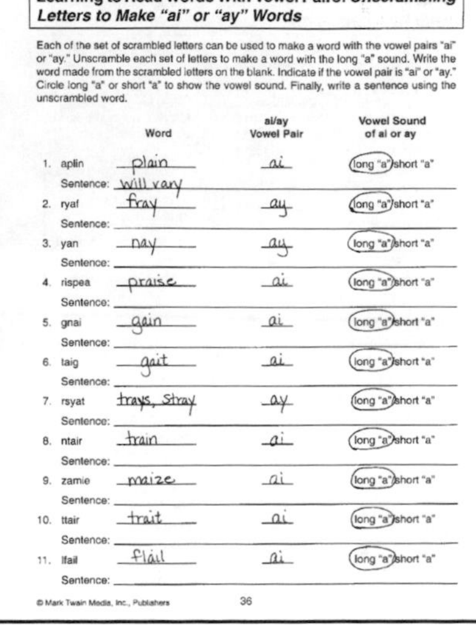

Phonics and Vocabulary Skills: Grade 5 — Unscrambling Letters to Make "ai" and "ay" Words

Name: ______ Date: ______

Learning to Read Words With Vowel Pairs: *Unscrambling Letters to Make "ai" or "ay" Words*

Each of the set of scrambled letters can be used to make a word with the vowel pairs "ai" or "ay." Unscramble each set of letters to make a word with the long "a" sound. Write the word made from the scrambled letters on the blank. Indicate if the vowel pair is "ai" or "ay." Circle long "a" or short "a" to show the vowel sound. Finally, write a sentence using the unscrambled word.

		Word	ai/ay Vowel Pair	Vowel Sound of ai or ay
1.	aplin	plain	ai	(long "a") short "a"
2.	ryaf	fray	ay	(long "a") short "a"
3.	yan	nay	ay	(long "a") short "a"
4.	rispea	praise	ai	(long "a") short "a"
5.	gnai	gain	ai	(long "a") short "a"
6.	taig	gait	ai	(long "a") short "a"
7.	rsyat	trays, stray	ay	(long "a") short "a"
8.	ntair	train	ai	(long "a") short "a"
9.	zamie	maize	ai	(long "a") short "a"
10.	ttair	trait	ai	(long "a") short "a"
11.	lfail	flail	ai	(long "a") short "a"

Sentence: will vary

© Mark Twain Media, Inc., Publishers 36

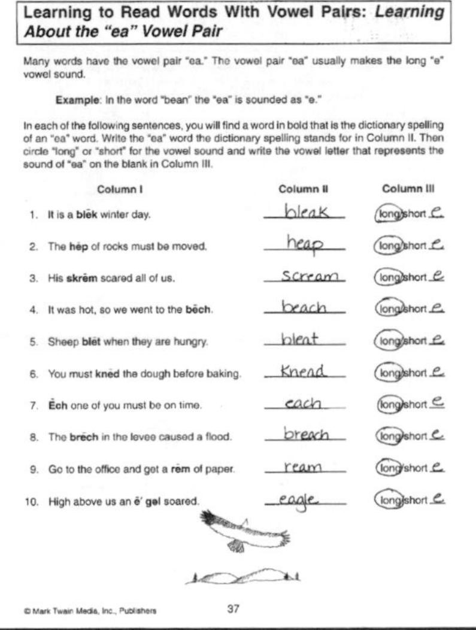

Phonics and Vocabulary Skills: Grade 5 — Learning About the "ea" Vowel Pair

Name: ______ Date: ______

Learning to Read Words With Vowel Pairs: *Learning About the "ea" Vowel Pair*

Many words have the vowel pair "ea." The vowel pair "ea" usually makes the long "e" vowel sound.

Example: In the word "bean" the "ea" is sounded as "e."

In each of the following sentences, you will find a word in bold that is the dictionary spelling of an "ea" word. Write the "ea" word the dictionary spelling stands for in Column II. Then circle "long" or "short" for the vowel sound and write the vowel letter that represents the sound of "ea" on the blank in Column III.

	Column I	Column II	Column III
1.	It is a **blēk** winter day.	bleak	(long) short e
2.	The **hēp** of rocks must be moved.	heap	(long) short e
3.	His **skrēm** scared all of us.	scream	(long) short e
4.	It was hot, so we went to the **bēch**.	beach	(long) short e
5.	Sheep **blēt** when they are hungry.	bleat	(long) short e
6.	You must **knēd** the dough before baking.	knead	(long) short e
7.	**Ēch** one of you must be on time.	each	(long) short e
8.	The **brēch** in the levee caused a flood.	breach	(long) short e
9.	Go to the office and get a **rēm** of paper.	ream	(long) short e
10.	High above us an **ē' gel** soared.	eagle	(long) short e

© Mark Twain Media, Inc., Publishers 37

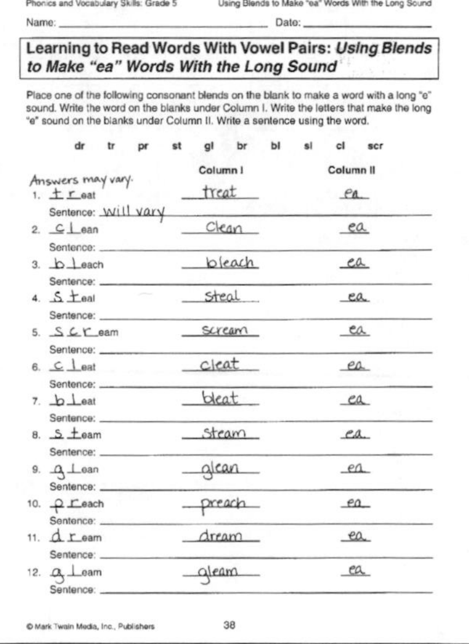

Phonics and Vocabulary Skills: Grade 5 — Using Blends to Make "ea" Words With the Long Sound

Name: ______ Date: ______

Learning to Read Words With Vowel Pairs: *Using Blends to Make "ea" Words With the Long Sound*

Place one of the following consonant blends on the blank to make a word with a long "e" sound. Write the word on the blanks under Column I. Write the letters that make the long "e" sound on the blanks under Column II. Write a sentence using the word.

dr tr pr st gl br bl sl cl scr

Answers may vary.

		Column I	Column II
1.	t r eat	treat	ea
2.	c l ean	clean	ea
3.	b l each	bleach	ea
4.	s t eal	steal	ea
5.	s c r eam	scream	ea
6.	c l eat	cleat	ea
7.	b l eat	bleat	ea
8.	s t eam	steam	ea
9.	g l ean	glean	ea
10.	p r each	preach	ea
11.	d r eam	dream	ea
12.	g l eam	gleam	ea

Sentence: will vary

© Mark Twain Media, Inc., Publishers 38

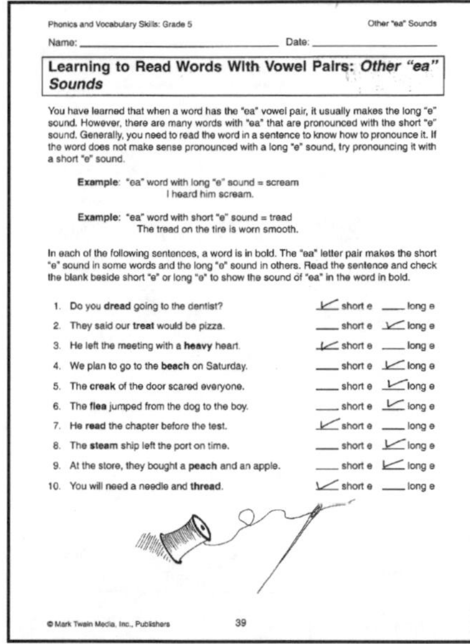

Phonics and Vocabulary Skills: Grade 5 — Other "ea" Sounds

Name: ____ Date: ____

Learning to Read Words With Vowel Pairs: *Other "ea" Sounds*

You have learned that when a word has the "ea" vowel pair, it usually makes the long "e" sound. However, there are many words with "ea" that are pronounced with the short "e" sound. Generally, you need to read the word in a sentence to know how to pronounce it. If the word does not make sense pronounced with a long "e" sound, try pronouncing it with a short "e" sound.

Example: "ea" word with long "e" sound = scream
I heard him scream.

Example: "ea" word with short "e" sound = tread
The tread on the tire is worn smooth.

In each of the following sentences, a word is in bold. The "ea" letter pair makes the short "e" sound in some words and the long "e" sound in others. Read the sentence and check the blank beside short "e" or long "e" to show the sound of "ea" in the word in bold.

1. Do you **dread** going to the dentist? ✓ short e ___ long e
2. They said our **treat** would be pizza. ___ short e ✓ long e
3. He left the meeting with a **heavy** heart. ✓ short e ___ long e
4. We plan to go to the **beach** on Saturday. ___ short e ✓ long e
5. The **creak** of the door scared everyone. ___ short e ✓ long e
6. The **flea** jumped from the dog to the boy. ___ short e ✓ long e
7. He **read** the chapter before the test. ✓ short e ___ long e
8. The **steam** ship left the port on time. ___ short e ✓ long e
9. At the store, they bought a **peach** and an apple. ___ short e ✓ long e
10. You will need a needle and **thread**. ✓ short e ___ long e

© Mark Twain Media, Inc., Publishers 39

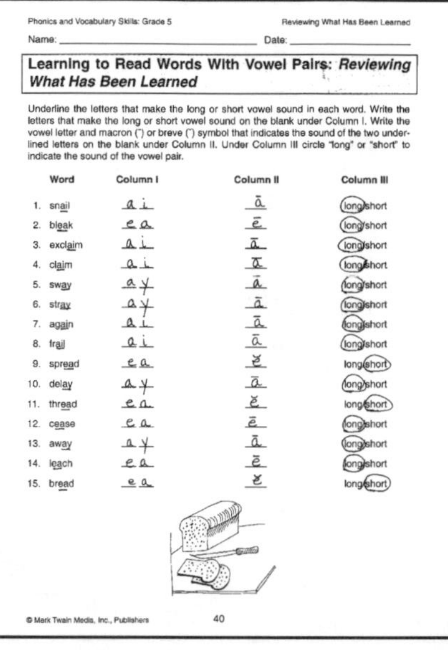

Phonics and Vocabulary Skills: Grade 5 — Reviewing What Has Been Learned

Name: ____ Date: ____

Learning to Read Words With Vowel Pairs: *Reviewing What Has Been Learned*

Underline the letters that make the long or short vowel sound in each word. Write the letters that make the long or short vowel sound on the blank under Column I. Write the vowel letter and macron (¯) or breve (˘) symbol that indicates the sound of the two underlined letters on the blank under Column II. Under Column III circle "long" or "short" to indicate the sound of the vowel pair.

	Word	Column I	Column II	Column III
1.	snail	ai	ā	(long)/short
2.	bleak	ea	ē	(long)/short
3.	exclaim	ai	ā	(long)/short
4.	claim	ai	ā	(long)/short
5.	sway	ay	ā	(long)/short
6.	stray	ay	ā	(long)/short
7.	again	ai	ā	(long)/short
8.	frail	ai	ā	(long)/short
9.	spread	ea	ĕ	long/(short)
10.	delay	ay	ā	(long)/short
11.	thread	ea	ĕ	long/(short)
12.	cease	ea	ē	(long)/short
13.	away	ay	ā	(long)/short
14.	leach	ea	ē	(long)/short
15.	bread	ea	ĕ	long/(short)

© Mark Twain Media, Inc., Publishers 40

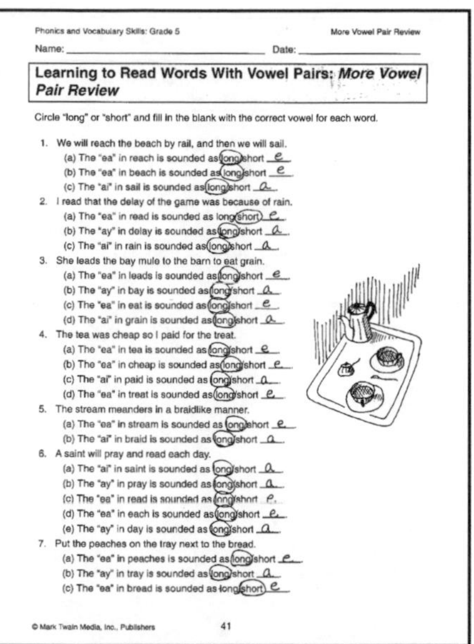

Phonics and Vocabulary Skills: Grade 5 — More Vowel Pair Review

Name: ____ Date: ____

Learning to Read Words With Vowel Pairs: *More Vowel Pair Review*

Circle "long" or "short" and fill in the blank with the correct vowel for each word.

1. We will reach the beach by rail, and then we will sail.
   (a) The "ea" in reach is sounded as (long)/short e
   (b) The "ea" in beach is sounded as (long)/short e
   (c) The "ai" in sail is sounded as (long)/short a
2. I read that the delay of the game was because of rain.
   (a) The "ea" in read is sounded as long/(short) e
   (b) The "ay" in delay is sounded as (long)/short a
   (c) The "ai" in rain is sounded as (long)/short a
3. She leads the bay mule to the barn to eat grain.
   (a) The "ea" in leads is sounded as (long)/short e
   (b) The "ay" in bay is sounded as (long)/short a
   (c) The "ea" in eat is sounded as (long)/short e
   (d) The "ai" in grain is sounded as (long)/short a
4. The tea was cheap so I paid for the treat.
   (a) The "ea" in tea is sounded as (long)/short e
   (b) The "ea" in cheap is sounded as (long)/short e
   (c) The "ai" in paid is sounded as (long)/short a
   (d) The "ea" in treat is sounded as (long)/short e
5. The stream meanders in a braidlike manner.
   (a) The "ea" in stream is sounded as (long)/short e
   (b) The "ai" in braid is sounded as (long)/short a
6. A saint will pray and read each day.
   (a) The "ai" in saint is sounded as (long)/short a
   (b) The "ay" in pray is sounded as (long)/short a
   (c) The "ea" in read is sounded as (long)/short e
   (d) The "ea" in each is sounded as (long)/short e
   (e) The "ay" in day is sounded as (long)/short a
7. Put the peaches on the tray next to the bread.
   (a) The "ea" in peaches is sounded as (long)/short e
   (b) The "ay" in tray is sounded as (long)/short a
   (c) The "ea" in bread is sounded as long/(short) e

© Mark Twain Media, Inc., Publishers 41

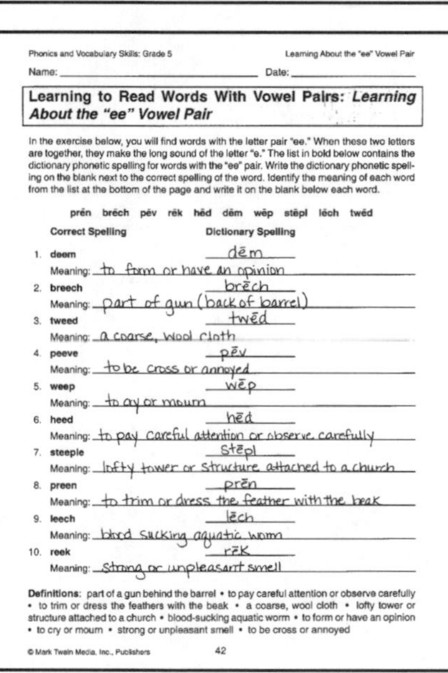

Phonics and Vocabulary Skills: Grade 5 — Learning About the "ee" Vowel Pair

Name: ____ Date: ____

Learning to Read Words With Vowel Pairs: *Learning About the "ee" Vowel Pair*

In the exercise below, you will find words with the letter pair "ee." When these two letters are together, they make the long sound of the letter "e." The list in bold below contains the dictionary phonetic spelling for words with the "ee" pair. Write the dictionary phonetic spelling on the blank next to the correct spelling of the word. Identify the meaning of each word from the list at the bottom of the page and write it on the blank below each word.

prēn brēch pēv rēk hēd dēm wēp stēpl lēch twēd

Correct Spelling — **Dictionary Spelling**

1. **deem** — dēm
   Meaning: to form or have an opinion
2. **breech** — brēch
   Meaning: part of gun (back of barrel)
3. **tweed** — twēd
   Meaning: a coarse, wool cloth
4. **peeve** — pēv
   Meaning: to be cross or annoyed
5. **weep** — wēp
   Meaning: to cry or mourn
6. **heed** — hēd
   Meaning: to pay careful attention or observe carefully
7. **steeple** — stēpl
   Meaning: lofty tower or structure attached to a church
8. **preen** — prēn
   Meaning: to trim or dress the feather with the beak
9. **leech** — lēch
   Meaning: blood sucking aquatic worm
10. **reek** — rēk
   Meaning: strong or unpleasant smell

Definitions: part of a gun behind the barrel • to pay careful attention or observe carefully • to trim or dress the feathers with the beak • a coarse, wool cloth • lofty tower or structure attached to a church • blood-sucking aquatic worm • to form or have an opinion • to cry or mourn • strong or unpleasant smell • to be cross or annoyed

© Mark Twain Media, Inc., Publishers 42

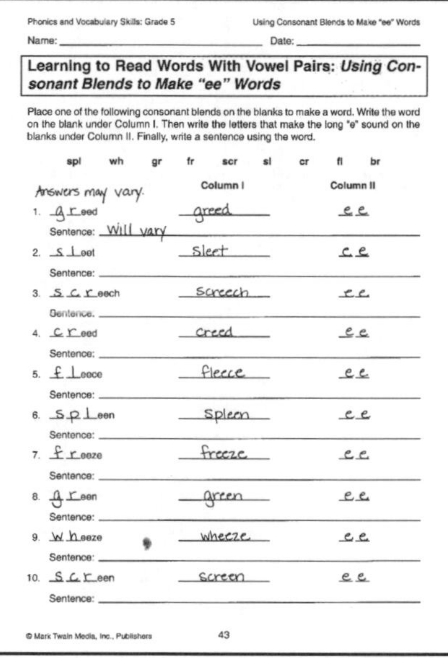

Phonics and Vocabulary Skills: Grade 5 — Using Consonant Blends to Make "ee" Words

Name: ____ Date: ____

Learning to Read Words With Vowel Pairs: *Using Consonant Blends to Make "ee" Words*

Place one of the following consonant blends on the blanks to make a word. Write the word on the blank under Column I. Then write the letters that make the long "e" sound on the blanks under Column II. Finally, write a sentence using the word.

spl wh gr fr scr sl cr fl br

Answers may vary.

		Column I	Column II
1.	g r eed	greed	e e
2.	s l eet	sleet	e e
3.	s c r eech	screech	e e
4.	c r eed	creed	e e
5.	f l eece	fleece	e e
6.	s p l een	spleen	e e
7.	f r eeze	freeze	e e
8.	g r een	green	e e
9.	w h eeze	wheeze	e e
10.	s c r een	screen	e e

Sentence: Will vary

© Mark Twain Media, Inc., Publishers 43

Phonics and Vocabulary Skills: Grade 5 — Reviewing Words With the Vowel Pairs "ai," "ay," "ea," or "ee"

Name: ____ Date: ____

Learning to Read Words With Vowel Pairs: *Reviewing Words With the Vowel Pairs "ai," "ay," "ea," or "ee"*

Circle the words in each sentence with the vowel pair "ai," "ay," "ea," or "ee."

1. The (maize) and (hay) are (feed) for the (beast).
2. The (faint) (queen) could not (read) the (speech).
3. The (steeple) of the church could be (seen) from the (street).
4. To make (bread) the (maid) must (knead) the dough and place it in a (tray).
5. (Today) many people have (great) (pain) and (weep) when their (team) is in the (fray).
6. It was a (great) (gray) (beast) from the (deep).
7. He (dreamed) the ship would (sail) through the (strait) and out to (sea).
8. I (read) that a (meal) for a small (fee) is a (real) (deal).
9. (Today) the (lean) (queen) ate a (meal) of (meat) and (maize).
10. He would (sneeze) and (wheeze) when the (hay) was baled.
11. The (snail) in the (pail) became a (meal).
12. Will (Ray) (deem) it necessary to (display) his (train) set at the show?
13. The (jail) (reeked) of (sweat) and (tears).
14. I would (weep) if a (leech) touched my (breeches).
15. (Spray) the (paint) from the (pail) on the (quaint) house by the (beach).

© Mark Twain Media, Inc., Publishers 44

Phonics and Vocabulary Skills: Grade 5 — Learning About the "oa" Vowel Pair

Name: ____ Date: ____

Learning to Read Words With Vowel Pairs: *Learning About the "oa" Vowel Pair*

The letter pair "oa" makes the long "o" sound. Place the following consonants on the blanks to make a word. Write the word on the blank under Column I. Write the letters that make the long "o" sound on the blank under Column II. Write a sentence using the word.

k c thr gl b fl br r

Answers may vary.

		Column I	Column II
1.	g l oat	gloat	oa
2.	f l oat	float	oa
3.	b oat	boat	oa
4.	b r oast	broast	oa
5.	b r oach	broach	oa
6.	c oach	coach	oa
7.	oa k	oak	oa
8.	t h r oat	throat	oa
9.	c oat	coat	oa
10.	b oast	boast	oa

Sentence: Will vary

© Mark Twain Media, Inc., Publishers 45

Phonics and Vocabulary Skills: Grade 5 — Unscrambling Letters to Make Words With the "oa" Vowel Pair

Name: ____ Date: ____

Learning to Read Words With Vowel Pairs: *Unscrambling Letters to Make Words With the "oa" Vowel Pair*

Unscramble the letters below to match the definition. Write the unscrambled word on the blank. Circle "long" or "short" and complete the blank to show the sound of the vowel.

		Scrambled Word	Unscrambled Word	Vowel Sound
1.	to brag	asbot	boast	(long)/short o
2.	to bake as in an oven	oarst	roast	(long)/short o
3.	a kind of tree	ako	oak	(long)/short o
4.	low sound made when in pain	naom	moan	(long)/short o
5.	to utter a sound like a frog	ckora	croak	(long)/short o
6.	land area near the ocean	tcaos	coast	(long)/short o
7.	passage from mouth to lungs	rhtota	throat	(long)/short o
8.	a kind of soil	mloa	loam	(long)/short o
9.	to take game or fish illegally	cohpa	poach	(long)/short o
10.	to persuade gently	xaco	coax	(long)/short o

Use each of the words above in a sentence.

1. Sentences will vary

© Mark Twain Media, Inc., Publishers 46

Phonics and Vocabulary Skills: Grade 5 — Reviewing What Has Been Learned

Name: ____ Date: ____

Learning to Read Words With Vowel Pairs: *Reviewing What Has Been Learned*

Read each of the following sentences. Read the directions by each sentence and write the answer on the blank below each sentence.

1. The man with the long mane began to boast.
   (Write the words that have short "a," long "a," and long "o" sounds.)
   man, began, mane, boast
2. Each day we went to the coast to see the boats sail.
   (Write the words with long "e," long "a," and long "o" sounds.)
   each, day, we, see, sail, coast, the, boats
3. The green yeast would make bread to toast.
   (Write the words with long "e," long "a," short "e," and long "o" sounds.)
   The, green, yeast, make, bread, toast
4. The moan of the coach was in vain as the team began to loaf.
   (Write the words with long "o," long "a," and long "e" sounds.)
   moan, coach, loaf, vain, team, the
5. I will spread butter on the bread.
   (Write the words with short "e" sounds.)
   spread, bread
6. The feather from the dead eagle lay on the beach.
   (Write the words with short "e," long "e," and long "a," sounds.)
   feather, dead, eagle, beach, lay, the
7. A frail male rode the mule.
   (Write the words with long "a," long "o," and long "u" sounds.)
   A, frail, male, rode, mule.
8. The dainty queen broached the subject.
   (Write the words with long "a," long "o," and long "e" sounds.)
   dainty, broached, the, queen
9. The wool from the wee sheep will be used to make tweed.
   (Write the words with long "e" and silent "e" sounds.)
   wee, sheep, tweed, make
10. Beef is the meat to braise or roast.
   (Write the words with long "e," long "a," and long "o" sound.)
   beef, meat, braize, roast, the

© Mark Twain Media, Inc., Publishers 47

Phonics and Vocabulary Skills: Grade 5 — Learning About the "ei" Vowel Pair

Name: ______ Date: ______

Learning About Words With the Vowel Pairs "ei," "ie," and "ey": *Learning About the "ei" Vowel Pair*

In many words that have a vowel combination, the first vowel is given the long sound and the second vowel is silent. In some words, the vowel sound is short rather than long. The best way to determine the sound of the these vowel combinations is to determine if the word in which the vowel combination is found makes sense in a sentence. If it doesn't, try the other sound to see if the new word makes sense.

The vowel pair "ei" is found in many words. In the words below the vowels "ei" will have the long sound of "e" as in *either* or the long "a" sound like "ei" in *eight*.

Example: either = long "e" sound **Example:** eight = long "a" sound

In each of the following sentences, the words with the "ei" vowels have the long sound of "e" or the long sound of "a." Read the sentences and determine the sound of the vowel pair. Place the word on the blank to show the sound of "ei." The first one has been completed for you. **Hint:** If you don't know how to pronounce a word, try both the long "e" and long "a" sound to see if either sound is a word you know.

	ei Word	Long e	Long a
1. Neither John nor Sam went to the game.	neither	e	
2. The woman with the beige hat sat quietly.	beige		a
3. We spent our leisure time jogging.	leisure	e	
4. If war starts, they will seize the island.	seize	e	
5. The freight will arrive by truck.	freight		a

Write a sentence using each of the following "ei" words. Also, complete the blanks to show the sound of "ei."

1. **protein** long e
   Sentence: will vary
2. **neighbor** long a
   Sentence:
3. **conceive** long e
   Sentence:
4. **rein** long a
   Sentence:
5. **sleigh** long a
   Sentence:

© Mark Twain Media, Inc., Publishers 48

Phonics and Vocabulary Skills: Grade 5 — Learning About the "ie" Vowel Pair

Name: ______ Date: ______

Learning About Words With the Vowel Pairs "ei," "ie," and "ey": *Learning About the "ie" Vowel Pair*

The "ie" vowel pair has the long "i" or long "e" sound in the word.

Example: The long sound of "i" is found in the word "die."
Example: The long sound of "e" is found in the word "field."

In each of the following sentences is a word with the "ie" vowel pair. Read each sentence and determine the sound of the "ie" pair. Complete the blanks. The first one has been completed for you. **Hint:** If you don't know how to pronounce a word, try both the long "i" and long "e" sound. See which sound gives a word you know.

	ie Word	Long i	Long e
1. The chief was at the fire station.	chief		e
2. He tried to complete the homework.	tried	i	
3. They have not replied to our letter.	replied	i	
4. Will they send relief supplies to help?	relief		e
5. Practice good hygiene by washing your hands.	hygiene		e
6. Rabies is common among wild animals.	rabies		e

Write a sentence using each of the following "ie" words. Also, complete the blanks to show the sound of "ie."

1. **piece** long e
   Sentence: will vary
2. **pried** long i
   Sentence:
3. **achieve** long e
   Sentence:
4. **spies** long i
   Sentence:
5. **shriek** long e
   Sentence:
6. **dried** long i
   Sentence:

© Mark Twain Media, Inc., Publishers 49

Phonics and Vocabulary Skills: Grade 5 — Learning About the "ey" Vowel Pair

Name: ______ Date: ______

Learning About Words With the Vowel Pairs "ei," "ie," and "ey": *Learning About the "ey" Vowel Pair*

In some words, the letter combination "ey" has a long "e" sound. In other words, the "ey" makes the long "a" sound.

Example: donkey = long "e" sound **Example:** hey = long "a" sound

Read each of the following sentences and circle the word with the "ey" vowel pair. Then place a check mark to indicate the vowel sound of the "ey" vowel pair. **Hint:** If a word doesn't make sense using one long sound, try the other long sound.

1. In the west, (they) grow a grain called (barley)	✓ long e	✓ long a
2. Many people now raise bees and sell the (honey)	✓ long e	__ long a
3. Do you have enough (money) for the movie?	✓ long e	__ long a
4. Cats (prey) on mice.	__ long e	✓ long a
5. The (monkey) was kept in a cage.	✓ long e	__ long a
6. Marco Polo's (journey) to China took many years.	✓ long e	__ long a
7. The winning (jockey) in the race was a woman.	✓ long e	__ long a
8. You must (obey) the rules in school.	__ long e	✓ long a
9. The glee club sang a (medley) of songs.	✓ long e	__ long a
10. Meals are prepared in the (galley) of the ship.	✓ long e	__ long a

Write a sentence using each of the following "ey" words. Also, complete the blanks to show the sound of "ey."

1. **hockey** long e
   Sentence: will vary
2. **hey** long a
   Sentence:
3. **they** long a
   Sentence:
4. **kidney** long e
   Sentence:
5. **convey** long a
   Sentence:

© Mark Twain Media, Inc., Publishers 50

Phonics and Vocabulary Skills: Grade 5 — Reviewing What Has Been Learned About "ei," "ie," "ay," and "ey"

Name: ______ Date: ______

Learning About Words With the Vowel Pairs "ei," "ie," and "ey": *Reviewing What Has Been Learned About "ei," "ie," "ay," and "ey"*

In each of the following sentences is a blank. Unscramble the letters at the end of each sentence to make a word with the vowel pair "ei," "ie," "ay," or "ey." Write the word on the blank to make a meaningful sentence. Then write what vowel sound the vowel pair makes.

		Vowel Sound
1. Golf is a leisure time sport.	**eislreu**	long e
2. Bears love to eat honey	**yonhe**	long e
3. In the Civil War, there were many spies.	**pises**	long i
4. Each of us must seize opportunities.	**eizes**	long e
5. To win we must play well.	**layp**	long a
6. The sunny day gave us a ray of hope.	**yra**	long a
7. The donkey is a beast of burden.	**kednoy**	long e
8. We should receive the package soon.	**eievrce**	long e
9. The priest was a kind man.	**riepts**	long e
10. Do you believe his story?	**elibeve**	long e
11. Roman soldiers carried a shield.	**hsldie**	long e
12. She wore a beige skirt.	**elgbe**	long a
13. After it snowed, we went for a sleigh ride.	**lsiehg**	long a
14. We must try hard to achieve our goal.	**chievae**	long e
15. The sailor tied the rope to the wharf.	**edit**	long i
16. Hey where do you think you are going?	**eyh**	long a
17. What was the winning time in the relay race?	**leray**	long a
18. Mom's apple pies were the best at the fair.	**sipe**	long i
19. Our neighbor just trimmed his bushes.	**ghnbroel**	long a
20. The jewelry was stolen by a thief.	**itehf**	long e

© Mark Twain Media, Inc., Publishers 51

Phonics and Vocabulary Skills: Grade 5 — Learning About the "oo" Vowel Pair

Name: ______ Date: ______

Learning About "oo," "au," "aw," and "ew": *Learning about the "oo" Vowel Pair*

The vowel pairs "oo," "au," "aw," and "ew" are found in many words. When these vowel pairs are found in a word, the sound is neither long or short.

In many words with the vowel pair "oo," the "oo" is sounded like "oo" in *boot*. In other words, the "oo" is sounded like the "oo" in *good*. Pronounce each of the following words aloud. Watch carefully how you make the "oo" sound. If the "oo" sounds like "oo" in *good*, place the word on a blank under **good**. If the "oo" sound like the "oo" in *boot*, place the word on a blank under **boot**.

roof	**root**	**book**	**shoot**	**spoon**	**nook**	**shook**
crook	**doom**	**room**	**poor**	**tooth**	**hoof**	**food**
cook	**noon**	**pool**	**loop**			

boot		good	
roof	pool	crook	shook
root	loop	cook	
doom	shoot	book	
noon	spoon	nook	
room	tooth	hoof	
food	poor		

Match each of the following words with the definition on the right.

g	1. nook	a. sound made by a train or ship
f	2. brood	b. sailing vessel
d	3. moor	c. produced by sheep
a	4. toot	d. land of poor drainage and wasteland in England
h	5. gloom	e. chess piece
j	6. hoop	f. number of small animals hatched at same time
e	7. rook	g. a corner in a room
i	8. brook	h. feeling of sadness
b	9. sloop	i. small stream
c	10. wool	j. circular band of metal or wood

© Mark Twain Media, Inc., Publishers 52

Phonics and Vocabulary Skills: Grade 5 — Using "oo" Words in Sentences

Name: ______ Date: ______

Learning About "oo," "au," "aw," and "ew": *Using "oo" Words in Sentences*

Complete the blanks in each of the following sentences using the words below.

brook gloom nook brood cool rook moor wool sloop toot

1. In England the moor is a land of poor drainage and wasteland.
2. She played the rook well and won the chess game.
3. A mother duck and her brood waddled toward the lake.
4. The cool breeze brought relief from the heat.
5. The bad news resulted in a feeling of gloom by all.
6. When we heard the toot of the train whistle, we were sad.
7. Although the room was large, they had only a nook for their own use.
8. We camped by a small mountain brook that bubbled and gurgled all night.
9. The wool from the sheep will be used to make shirts.
10. Late at night, the sloop quietly sailed into the open sea.

Use one of the following consonants in each blank to make a word that completes the meaning of the sentence.

sch b sm l h m sh sp g n sl bl br w r c cr tr st

1. The flowers by the brook will bloom in the fall.
2. By the creek was the hoof print left by the moose.
3. The spool of wool will be used to make a shirt.
4. They wrote a book about the goose who was loose.
5. In the nook of the room he sat by himself.
6. He went to school to learn how to make cookies.
7. A smooth crook is hard to catch.
8. When the bugle sounded, the troop stood ready for inspection.
9. Across the moor a cool breeze blew.
10. The sloop shook as it began to sail out to sea.

© Mark Twain Media, Inc., Publishers 53

Phonics and Vocabulary Skills: Grade 5 — Reviewing What Has Been Learned

Name: ______ Date: ______

Learning About "oo," "au," "aw," and "ew": *Reviewing What Has Been Learned*

Read each of the following sentences. Follow the directions for each sentence. Write a sentence using the words written on the blanks.

1. I looked through the pane and saw a lame moose. (Write the words with a silent "e".)
   looked, pane, lame, moose
   Sentence: will vary
   Sentence:
   Sentence:
2. The animal with a white stripe left a vile smell. (Write the words with a silent "e" and a long "i" sound.)
   white, stripe, vile
   Sentence:
   Sentence:
   Sentence:
3. On the throne in a robe sat the king with a phone. (Write the words with a long "o" and a silent "e".)
   throne, robe, phone
   Sentence:
   Sentence:
   Sentence:
4. A dude with a flute played a tune. (Write the words with a long "u" and a silent "e".)
   dude, flute, tune
   Sentence:
   Sentence:
   Sentence:
5. In the chaise rode a frail maid. (Write the words with "ai" and a long "a" sound.)
   chaise, frail, maid
   Sentence:
   Sentence:
   Sentence:

© Mark Twain Media, Inc., Publishers 54

Phonics and Vocabulary Skills: Grade 5 — Reviewing What Has Been Learned

Name: ______ Date: ______

Learning About "oo," "au," "aw," and "ew": *Reviewing What Has Been Learned (continued)*

6. The dray was loaded with gray clay. (Write the words with "ay" and a long "a" sound.)
   dray, gray, clay
   Sentence:
   Sentence:
   Sentence:
7. The bleach left a streak on the pleat. (Write the words with "ea" and a long "e" sound.)
   bleach, streak, pleat
   Sentence:
   Sentence:
   Sentence:
8. Tweed is made from the fleece of a sheep. (Write the words with "ee" and a long "e" sound.)
   tweed, fleece, sheep
   Sentence:
   Sentence:
   Sentence:
9. The goal was to coax a moan from the goat. (Write the words with "oa" and a long "o" sound.)
   goal, coax, moan, goat
   Sentence:
   Sentence:
   Sentence:
   Sentence:
10. In the zoo a goose stood on one foot by the pool. (Write the words with the "oo" sound under the words "doom" or "hook" below with the same "oo" sound.)

doom	hook
zoo	stood
goose	foot
pool	

© Mark Twain Media, Inc., Publishers 55

Phonics and Vocabulary Skills: Grade 5 — Learning About "au" and "aw" Words

Name: ______ Date: ______

Learning About "oo," "au," "aw," and "ew": *Learning About "au" and "aw" Words*

The letter pairs "au" and "aw" are found in many words. These two letter pairs make the sound "aw" in words where they are found. The following are some words with the "au" or "aw" letter pairs.

Complete the blank in each sentence using a word from the list below.

applause shawl brawl launch caustic prawn thaw laundry gauze caw

1. They plan to launch the rocket today.
2. She wore a blue shawl around her shoulders
3. It was so warm we were afraid the ice would thaw.
4. A brawl is not a sign of manhood.
5. His caustic remarks hurt my feelings.
6. Another word for shrimp is prawn.
7. We had to do our laundry before leaving on the trip.
8. The speaker knew the crowd was pleased when the applause went on for five minutes.
9. In case there is an accident, we will take tape and gauze on our camping trip.
10. The caw from the crow frightened the other animals.

Unscramble the following letters to make a word with the letter pair "au" or "aw." Use the word in a sentence.

1. untag gaunt
   Sentence: will vary
2. ttnau taunt
   Sentence:
3. aldrw drawl
   Sentence:
4. npswa spawn
   Sentence:
5. rudfa fraud
   Sentence:

© Mark Twain Media, Inc., Publishers 56

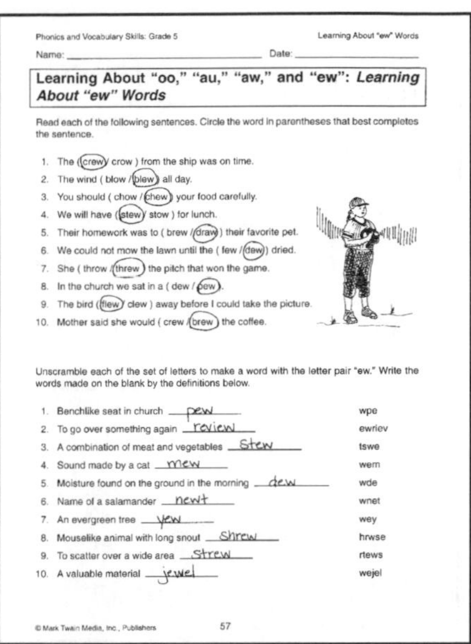

Phonics and Vocabulary Skills: Grade 5 | Learning About "ew" Words

Name: ______ Date: ______

Learning About "oo," "au," "aw," and "ew": ***Learning About "ew" Words***

Read each of the following sentences. Circle the word in parentheses that best completes the sentence.

1. The (crew / crow) from the ship was on time. (crew)
2. The wind (blow / blew) all day. (blew)
3. You should (chow / chew) your food carefully. (chew)
4. We will have (stew / stow) for lunch. (stew)
5. Their homework was to (brew / draw) their favorite pet. (draw)
6. We could not mow the lawn until the (few / dew) dried. (dew)
7. She (throw / threw) the pitch that won the game. (threw)
8. In the church we sat in a (dew / pew). (pew)
9. The bird (flew / clew) away before I could take the picture. (flew)
10. Mother said she would (crew / brew) the coffee. (brew)

Unscramble each of the set of letters to make a word with the letter pair "ew." Write the words made on the blank by the definitions below.

	Definition	Answer	Letters
1.	Benchlike seat in church	pew	wpe
2.	To go over something again	review	ewriev
3.	A combination of meat and vegetables	Stew	tswe
4.	Sound made by a cat	mew	wem
5.	Moisture found on the ground in the morning	dew	wde
6.	Name of a salamander	newt	wnet
7.	An evergreen tree	yew	wey
8.	Mouselike animal with long snout	Shrew	hrwse
9.	To scatter over a wide area	Strew	rtews
10.	A valuable material	jewel	wejel

© Mark Twain Media, Inc., Publishers 57

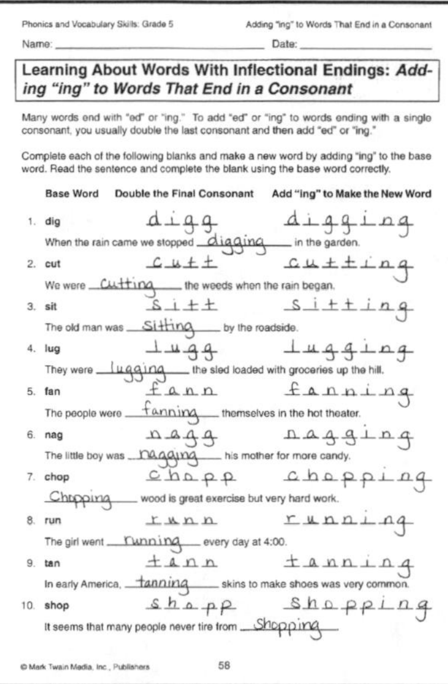

Phonics and Vocabulary Skills: Grade 5 | Adding "ing" to Words That End in a Consonant

Name: ______ Date: ______

Learning About Words With Inflectional Endings: ***Adding "ing" to Words That End in a Consonant***

Many words end with "ed" or "ing." To add "ed" or "ing" to words ending with a single consonant, you usually double the last consonant and then add "ed" or "ing."

Complete each of the following blanks and make a new word by adding "ing" to the base word. Read the sentence and complete the blank using the base word correctly.

	Base Word	Double the Final Consonant	Add "ing" to Make the New Word
1.	dig	digg	digging
2.	cut	cutt	cutting
3.	sit	sitt	sitting
4.	lug	lugg	lugging
5.	fan	fann	fanning
6.	nag	nagg	nagging
7.	chop	chopp	chopping
8.	run	runn	running
9.	tan	tann	tanning
10.	shop	shopp	shopping

1. When the rain came we stopped digging in the garden.
2. We were Cutting the weeds when the rain began.
3. The old man was Sitting by the roadside.
4. They were lugging the sled loaded with groceries up the hill.
5. The people were fanning themselves in the hot theater.
6. The little boy was nagging his mother for more candy.
7. Chopping wood is great exercise but very hard work.
8. The girl went running every day at 4:00.
9. In early America, tanning skins to make shoes was very common.
10. It seems that many people never tire from Shopping.

© Mark Twain Media, Inc., Publishers 58

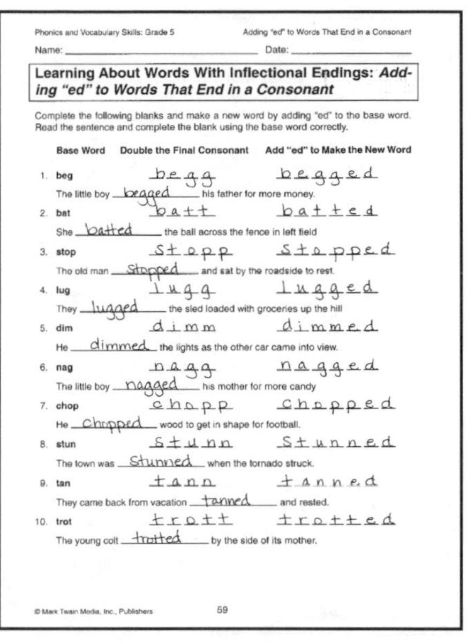

Phonics and Vocabulary Skills: Grade 5 | Adding "ed" to Words That End in a Consonant

Name: ______ Date: ______

Learning About Words With Inflectional Endings: ***Adding "ed" to Words That End in a Consonant***

Complete the following blanks and make a new word by adding "ed" to the base word. Read the sentence and complete the blank using the base word correctly.

	Base Word	Double the Final Consonant	Add "ed" to Make the New Word
1.	beg	begg	begged
2.	bat	batt	batted
3.	stop	stopp	stopped
4.	lug	lugg	lugged
5.	dim	dimm	dimmed
6.	nag	nagg	nagged
7.	chop	chopp	chopped
8.	stun	stunn	stunned
9.	tan	tann	tanned
10.	trot	trott	trotted

1. The little boy begged his father for more money.
2. She batted the ball across the fence in left field
3. The old man Stopped and sat by the roadside to rest.
4. They lugged the sled loaded with groceries up the hill
5. He dimmed the lights as the other car came into view.
6. The little boy nagged his mother for more candy
7. He Chopped wood to get in shape for football.
8. The town was Stunned when the tornado struck.
9. They came back from vacation tanned and rested.
10. The young colt trotted by the side of its mother.

© Mark Twain Media, Inc., Publishers 59

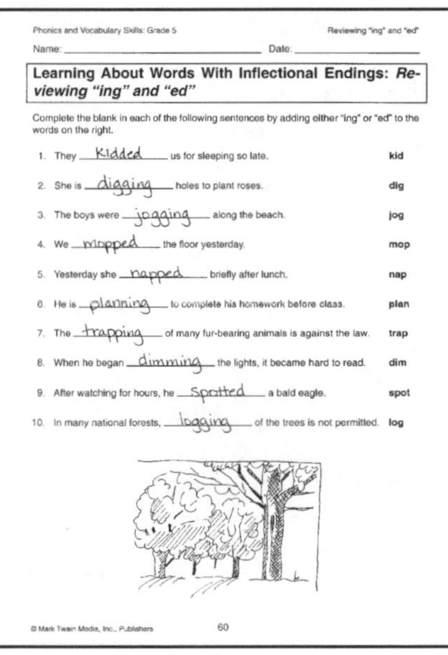

Phonics and Vocabulary Skills: Grade 5 | Reviewing "ing" and "ed"

Name: ______ Date: ______

Learning About Words With Inflectional Endings: ***Reviewing "ing" and "ed"***

Complete the blank in each of the following sentences by adding either "ing" or "ed" to the words on the right.

1. They Kidded us for sleeping so late. **kid**
2. She is digging holes to plant roses. **dig**
3. The boys were jogging along the beach. **jog**
4. We mopped the floor yesterday. **mop**
5. Yesterday she napped briefly after lunch. **nap**
6. He is planning to complete his homework before class. **plan**
7. The trapping of many fur-bearing animals is against the law. **trap**
8. When he began dimming the lights, it became hard to read. **dim**
9. After watching for hours, he Spotted a bald eagle. **spot**
10. In many national forests, logging of the trees is not permitted. **log**

© Mark Twain Media, Inc., Publishers 60

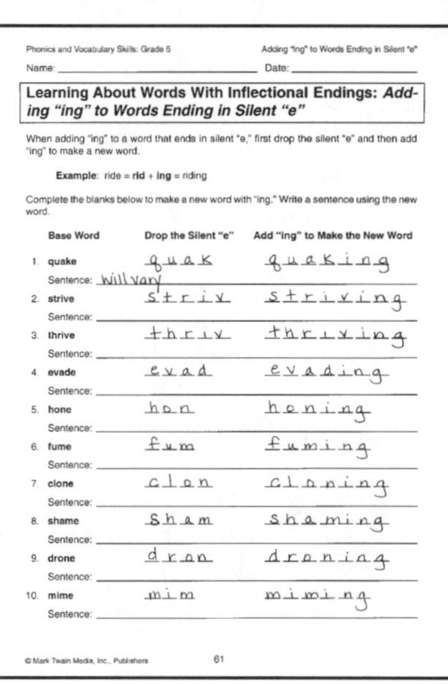

Phonics and Vocabulary Skills: Grade 5 | Adding "ing" to Words Ending in Silent "e"

Name: ______ Date: ______

Learning About Words With Inflectional Endings: ***Adding "ing" to Words Ending in Silent "e"***

When adding "ing" to a word that ends in silent "e," first drop the silent "e" and then add "ing" to make a new word.

Example: ride = **rid** + **ing** = riding

Complete the blanks below to make a new word with "ing." Write a sentence using the new word.

	Base Word	Drop the Silent "e"	Add "ing" to Make the New Word
1.	quake	quak	quaking
2.	strive	striv	striving
3.	thrive	thriv	thriving
4.	evade	evad	evading
5.	hone	hon	honing
6.	fume	fum	fuming
7.	clone	clon	cloning
8.	shame	sham	shaming
9.	drone	dron	droning
10.	mime	mim	miming

Sentence: Will vary

© Mark Twain Media, Inc., Publishers 61

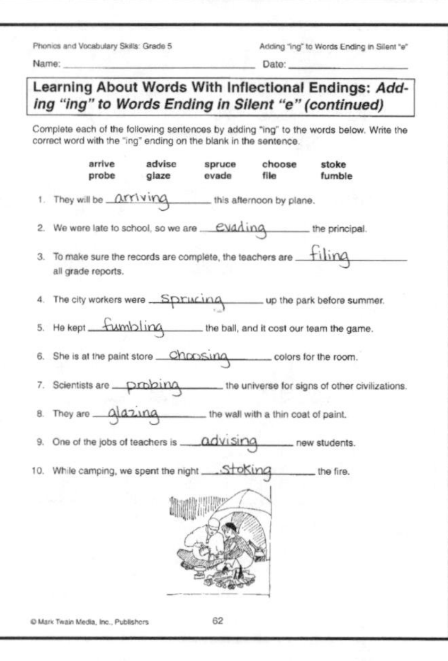

Phonics and Vocabulary Skills: Grade 5 | Adding "ing" to Words Ending in Silent "e"

Name: ______ Date: ______

Learning About Words With Inflectional Endings: ***Adding "ing" to Words Ending in Silent "e" (continued)***

Complete each of the following sentences by adding "ing" to the words below. Write the correct word with the "ing" ending on the blank in the sentence.

arrive **advise** **spruce** **choose** **stoke**
probe **glaze** **evade** **file** **fumble**

1. They will be arriving this afternoon by plane.
2. We were late to school, so we are evading the principal.
3. To make sure the records are complete, the teachers are filing all grade reports.
4. The city workers were Sprucing up the park before summer.
5. He kept fumbling the ball, and it cost our team the game.
6. She is at the paint store choosing colors for the room.
7. Scientists are probing the universe for signs of other civilizations.
8. They are glazing the wall with a thin coat of paint.
9. One of the jobs of teachers is advising new students.
10. While camping, we spent the night stoking the fire.

© Mark Twain Media, Inc., Publishers 62

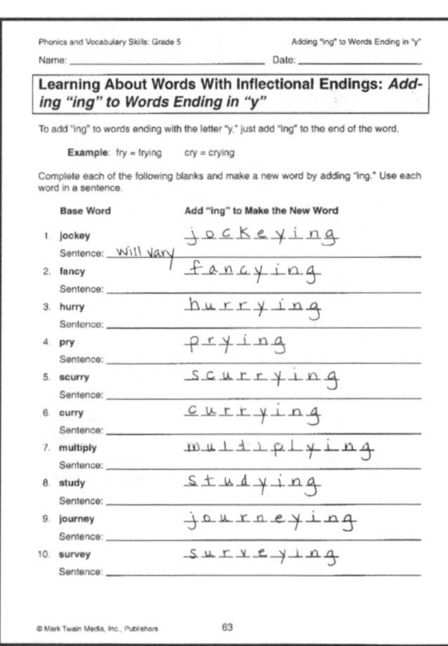

Phonics and Vocabulary Skills: Grade 5 | Adding "ing" to Words Ending in "y"

Name: ______ Date: ______

Learning About Words With Inflectional Endings: ***Adding "ing" to Words Ending in "y"***

To add "ing" to words ending with the letter "y," just add "ing" to the end of the word.

Example: fry = frying cry = crying

Complete each of the following blanks and make a new word by adding "ing." Use each word in a sentence.

	Base Word	Add "ing" to Make the New Word
1.	jockey	jockeying
2.	fancy	fancying
3.	hurry	hurrying
4.	pry	prying
5.	scurry	scurrying
6.	curry	currying
7.	multiply	multiplying
8.	study	studying
9.	journey	journeying
10.	survey	surveying

Sentence: Will vary

© Mark Twain Media, Inc., Publishers 63

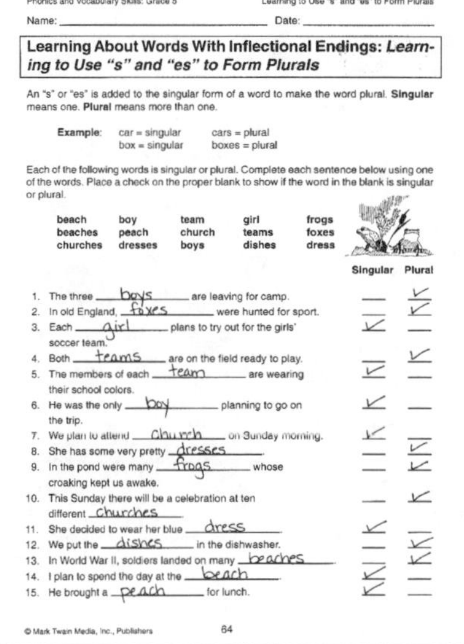

Phonics and Vocabulary Skills: Grade 5 | Learning to Use "s" and "es" to Form Plurals

Name: ______ Date: ______

Learning About Words With Inflectional Endings: ***Learning to Use "s" and "es" to Form Plurals***

An "s" or "es" is added to the singular form of a word to make the word plural. **Singular** means one. **Plural** means more than one.

Example: car = singular cars = plural
box = singular boxes = plural

Each of the following words is singular or plural. Complete each sentence below using one of the words. Place a check on the proper blank to show if the word in the blank is singular or plural.

beach **boy** **team** **girl** **frogs**
beaches **peach** **church** **teams** **foxes**
churches **dresses** **boys** **dishes** **dress**

	Sentence	Singular	Plural
1.	The three boys are leaving for camp.		✓
2.	In old England, foxes were hunted for sport.		✓
3.	Each girl plans to try out for the girls' soccer team.	✓	
4.	Both teams are on the field ready to play.		✓
5.	The members of each team are wearing their school colors.	✓	
6.	He was the only boy planning to go on the trip.	✓	
7.	We plan to attend Church on Sunday morning.	✓	
8.	She has some very pretty dresses.		✓
9.	In the pond were many frogs whose croaking kept us awake.		✓
10.	This Sunday there will be a celebration at ten different Churches.		✓
11.	She decided to wear her blue dress.	✓	
12.	We put the dishes in the dishwasher.		✓
13.	In World War II, soldiers landed on many beaches.		✓
14.	I plan to spend the day at the beach.	✓	
15.	He brought a peach for lunch.	✓	

© Mark Twain Media, Inc., Publishers 64

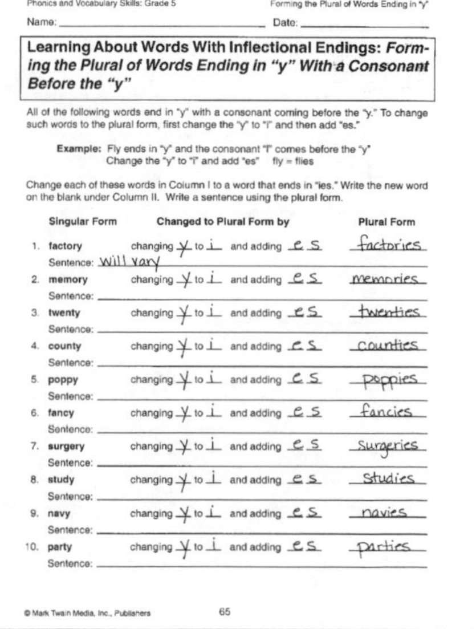

Phonics and Vocabulary Skills: Grade 5 | Forming the Plural of Words Ending in "y"

Name: ______ Date: ______

Learning About Words With Inflectional Endings: ***Forming the Plural of Words Ending in "y" With a Consonant Before the "y"***

All of the following words end in "y" with a consonant coming before the "y." To change such words to the plural form, first change the "y" to "i" and then add "es."

Example: Fly ends in "y" and the consonant "l" comes before the "y"
Change the "y" to "i" and add "es" fly = flies

Change each of these words in Column I to a word that ends in "ies." Write the new word on the blank under Column II. Write a sentence using the plural form.

	Singular Form	Changed to Plural Form by	Plural Form
1.	factory	changing y to i and adding es	factories
2.	memory	changing y to i and adding es	memories
3.	twenty	changing y to i and adding es	twenties
4.	county	changing y to i and adding es	counties
5.	poppy	changing y to i and adding es	poppies
6.	fancy	changing y to i and adding es	fancies
7.	surgery	changing y to i and adding es	surgeries
8.	study	changing y to i and adding es	studies
9.	navy	changing y to i and adding es	navies
10.	party	changing y to i and adding es	parties

Sentence: Will vary

© Mark Twain Media, Inc., Publishers 65

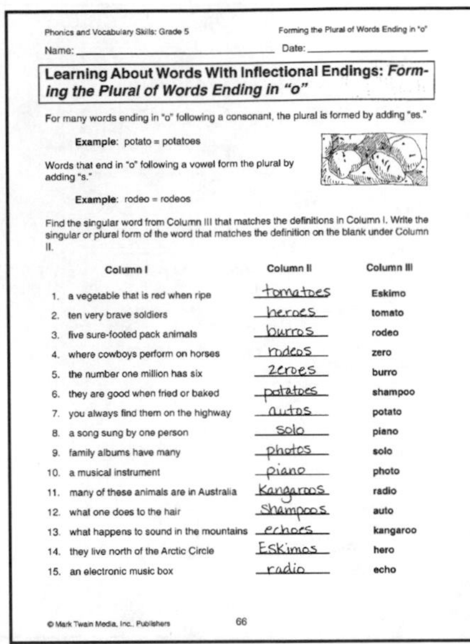

Phonics and Vocabulary Skills: Grade 5 — Forming the Plural of Words Ending in "o"

Name: ____ Date: ____

Learning About Words With Inflectional Endings: ***Forming the Plural of Words Ending in "o"***

For many words ending in "o" following a consonant, the plural is formed by adding "es."

Example: potato = potatoes

Words that end in "o" following a vowel form the plural by adding "s."

Example: rodeo = rodeos

Find the singular word from Column III that matches the definitions in Column I. Write the singular or plural form of the word that matches the definition on the blank under Column II.

Column I	Column II	Column III
1. a vegetable that is red when ripe	tomatoes	Eskimo
2. ten very brave soldiers	heroes	tomato
3. five sure-footed pack animals	burros	rodeo
4. where cowboys perform on horses	rodeos	zero
5. the number one million has six	zeroes	burro
6. they are good when fried or baked	potatoes	shampoo
7. you always find them on the highway	autos	potato
8. a song sung by one person	solo	piano
9. family albums have many	photos	solo
10. a musical instrument	piano	photo
11. many of these animals are in Australia	Kangaroos	radio
12. what one does to the hair	Shampoos	auto
13. what happens to sound in the mountains	echoes	kangaroo
14. they live north of the Arctic Circle	Eskimos	hero
15. an electronic music box	radio	echo

© Mark Twain Media, Inc., Publishers 66

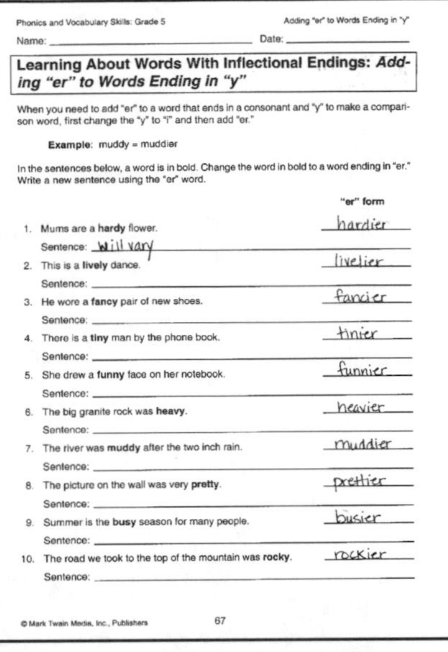

Phonics and Vocabulary Skills: Grade 5 — Adding "er" to Words Ending in "y"

Name: ____ Date: ____

Learning About Words With Inflectional Endings: ***Adding "er" to Words Ending in "y"***

When you need to add "er" to a word that ends in a consonant and "y" to make a comparison word, first change the "y" to "i" and then add "er."

Example: muddy = muddier

In the sentences below, a word is in bold. Change the word in bold to a word ending in "er." Write a new sentence using the "er" word.

	"er" form
1. Mums are a **hardy** flower. Sentence: will vary	hardier
2. This is a **lively** dance. Sentence:	livelier
3. He wore a **fancy** pair of new shoes. Sentence:	fancier
4. There is a **tiny** man by the phone book. Sentence:	tinier
5. She drew a **funny** face on her notebook. Sentence:	funnier
6. The big granite rock was **heavy**. Sentence:	heavier
7. The river was **muddy** after the two inch rain. Sentence:	muddier
8. The picture on the wall was very **pretty**. Sentence:	prettier
9. Summer is the **busy** season for many people. Sentence:	busier
10. The road we took to the top of the mountain was **rocky**. Sentence:	rockier

© Mark Twain Media, Inc., Publishers 67

Phonics and Vocabulary Skills: Grade 5 — Adding "est" to Words Ending in "y"

Name: ____ Date: ____

Learning About Words With Inflectional Endings: ***Adding "est" to Words Ending in "y"***

To add "est" to a word ending in a consonant and the letter "y," first change the "y" to an "i" and then add "est."

In the sentences below, a word is in bold that ends in "y." In each word, a consonant comes before the "y." Make a new word by changing the "y" to "i" and adding "est." Place the new word on the blank following each sentence. Write a sentence using the new "est" word.

	"est" word
1. He is **happy** now that his friends are back. Sentence: will vary	happiest
2. They told some very **funny** stories. Sentence:	funniest
3. She decided to buy the **pretty** blue skirt. Sentence:	prettiest
4. He left the **muddy** pair of boots by the door. Sentence:	muddiest
5. I think math is **easy** in the first hour class. Sentence:	easiest
6. He is **grumpy** in the morning. Sentence:	grumpiest
7. The big truck carries a **heavy** load. Sentence:	heaviest
8. He caught an **ugly** catfish and a beautiful trout. Sentence:	ugliest
9. Many **hardy** wildflowers are in need of rain. Sentence:	hardiest

© Mark Twain Media, Inc., Publishers 68

Phonics and Vocabulary Skills: Grade 5 — Adding "er" and "est" to Make New Words

Name: ____ Date: ____

Learning About Words With Inflectional Endings: ***Adding "er" and "est" to Make New Words***

Add "er" and "est" to each of the base words to make new words. Write the "er" and "est" words on the appropriate blanks.

Base Word	Base Word + "er"	Base Word + "est"
1. smooth	smoother	smoothest
2. clean	cleaner	cleanest
3. high	higher	highest
4. fast	faster	fastest
5. light	lighter	lightest
6. low	lower	lowest
7. sharp	sharper	sharpest
8. strong	stronger	strongest
9. cold	colder	coldest
10. bright	brighter	brightest

Each of the following words ends with a consonant with a vowel before the consonant. Double the consonant and add "er" and "est" to each of the base words. Write the "er" and "est" words on the blanks.

Base Word	Base Word + "er"	Base Word + "est"
1. hot	hotter	hottest
2. sad	sadder	saddest
3. fat	fatter	fattest
4. mad	madder	maddest
5. flat	flatter	flattest
6. wet	wetter	wettest
7. fit	fitter	fittest
8. red	redder	reddest

© Mark Twain Media, Inc., Publishers 69

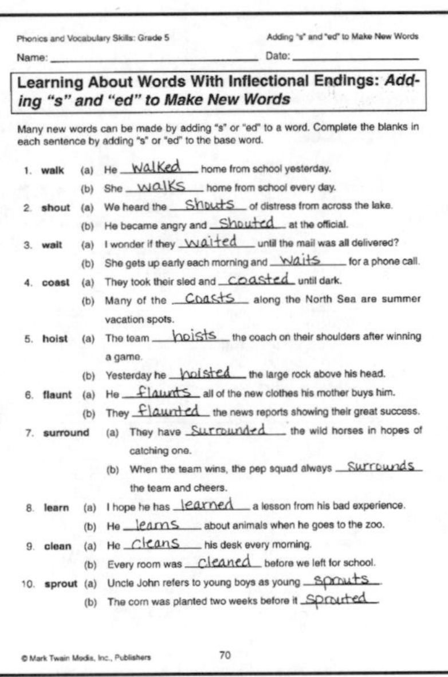

Phonics and Vocabulary Skills: Grade 5 — Adding "s" and "ed" to Make New Words

Name: ____ Date: ____

Learning About Words With Inflectional Endings: ***Adding "s" and "ed" to Make New Words***

Many new words can be made by adding "s" or "ed" to a word. Complete the blanks in each sentence by adding "s" or "ed" to the base word.

1. **walk** (a) He walked home from school yesterday. (b) She walks home from school every day.
2. **shout** (a) We heard the shouts of distress from across the lake. (b) He became angry and shouted at the official.
3. **wait** (a) I wonder if they waited until the mail was all delivered? (b) She gets up early each morning and waits for a phone call.
4. **coast** (a) They took their sled and coasted until dark. (b) Many of the coasts along the North Sea are summer vacation spots.
5. **hoist** (a) The team hoists the coach on their shoulders after winning a game. (b) Yesterday he hoisted the large rock above his head.
6. **flaunt** (a) He flaunts all of the new clothes his mother buys him. (b) They flaunted the news reports showing their great success.
7. **surround** (a) They have surrounded the wild horses in hopes of catching one. (b) When the team wins, the pep squad always surrounds the team and cheers.
8. **learn** (a) I hope he has learned a lesson from his bad experience. (b) He learns about animals when he goes to the zoo.
9. **clean** (a) He cleans his desk every morning. (b) Every room was cleaned before we left for school.
10. **sprout** (a) Uncle John refers to young boys as young sprouts. (b) The corn was planted two weeks before it sprouted.

© Mark Twain Media, Inc., Publishers 70

Phonics and Vocabulary Skills: Grade 5 — Learning About the Sounds of "ed"

Name: ____ Date: ____

Learning About Words With Inflectional Endings: ***Learning About the Sounds of "ed"***

When the inflection "ed" is added to a base word, the "ed" may be sounded as **/ed/**, **/t/**, or **/d/**. When "ed" is added to a base word that ends in "d" or "t," the "ed" is sounded as **/ed/**.

Example: plant + ed = planted = /ed/ sound

When the inflection "ed" is added to a base word not ending in "d" or "t," the sound of "ed" may be /d/ or /t/.

Examples: kick + ed = kicked = /t/ sound; fish + ed = fished = /d/ sound

Each sentence below has a word in bold. Read each of the sentences and write "ed," "t," or "d" on the blank above the inflection to show the correct sound of the inflection.

1. Many native American Indians lived in one area and **planted** (ed) corn each spring.
2. Many native American Indians **hunted** (ed) animals.
3. He **wanted** (ed) to make sure everyone was prepared for the test.
4. The band **played** (d) for over an hour.
5. When he heard the noise, he **jumped** (t) to his feet.
6. The principal said he **wished** (d) the school year was longer.
7. The artist **painted** (ed) beautiful scenes while relaxing at the beach.
8. In early America, young people **worked** very hard.
9. During World War II, marines **landed** (ed) on the beaches of France.
10. In early America, all members of the family **helped** (d) with the daily chores.

© Mark Twain Media, Inc., Publishers 71

Phonics and Vocabulary Skills: Grade 5 — Reviewing Inflections

Name: ____ Date: ____

Learning About Words With Inflectional Endings: ***Reviewing Inflections***

Each of the sentences has a word in bold followed by a blank. Write the correct form of the word on the blank below the word in bold. The first one has been completed for you.

1. The roses **plant**___ (planted) in the spring are blooming. We are now **plant**___ (planting) fall flowers.
2. We **hurry**___ (hurried) to catch the train. When we got to the station others were **hurry**___ (hurrying) to catch the same train.
3. The **small**___ (smallest) of the three brothers was ten years old. The other two brothers were **large**___ (larger).
4. The **hardy**___ (hardiest) flowers can stand cold weather. Some flowers are **hardy**___ (hardier) than others.
5. In war, bridges and buildings are **destroy**___ (destroyed). War often **destroy**___ (destroys) the history of a people.
6. Many of the people were on the streets where they **beg**___ (begged) for food. Some of those **beg**___ (beggars) were homeless.
7. The band included seven **flute**___ (flutists) and two **piano**___ (pianists).
8. Ten seventh-grade **girl**___ (girls) made the soccer team that plays today. The **play**___ (players) from both teams will be introduced before the game.
9. John is the **slow**___ (slower) of the two runners. He is not the **slow**___ (slowest) runner on the track team.
10. The cook was **fry**___ (frying) the potatoes. Everyone was wanting french **fry**___ (fries).

© Mark Twain Media, Inc., Publishers 72

Phonics and Vocabulary Skills: Grade 5 — Finding Root Words in Compound Words

Name: ____ Date: ____

Learning About Compound Words: ***Finding Root Words in Compound Words***

Compound words are words that include two root words. For example, the root words **any** and **one** form the compound word **anyone**.

Example: out + side = outside; home + town = hometown

Each of the following words is a compound word. Write the root words on the blanks. Then write a sentence using the compound word. The first one has been partially completed for you.

Compound Word	Root Word	Root Word
1. alongside (Sentence: will vary)	along	side
2. framework	frame	work
3. everything	every	thing
4. mainland	main	land
5. downstream	down	stream
6. furthermore	further	more
7. commonplace	common	place
8. boldface	bold	face
9. businessmen	business	men
10. farewell	fare	well

© Mark Twain Media, Inc., Publishers 73

Phonics and Vocabulary Skills: Grade 5 — Finding Compound Words in Sentences

Name: ____ Date: ____

Learning About Compound Words: ***Finding Compound Words in Sentences***

Each of the following sentences contains one or more compound words. Underline the compound words and write the roots on the blanks after the sentence.

	Root 1	Root 2
1. The goldfish must not be fed too much food.	gold	fish
2. When the new school is built, sandstone will be used for the foundation.	sand	stone
3. Be sure to clean the room, otherwise we will be late getting away.	other	wise
4. We must make sure that eating a balanced meal is widespread.	wide	spread
5. Many townspeople were without the needed protection from the storm.	towns	people
	with	out
6. Everybody thought the quarterback should pass more.	every	body
	quarter	back
7. The newspaper reported that the homework was common.	news	paper
	home	work
8. In the schoolhouse there were many textbooks that were for classroom use only.	school	house
	text	books
	class	room
9. The summertime thunderstorm came from the southeast.	summer	time
	thunder	storm
	south	east
10. Many cowboys dressed in buckskin whenever they were on the range.	cow	boys
	buck	skin
	when	ever

© Mark Twain Media, Inc., Publishers 74

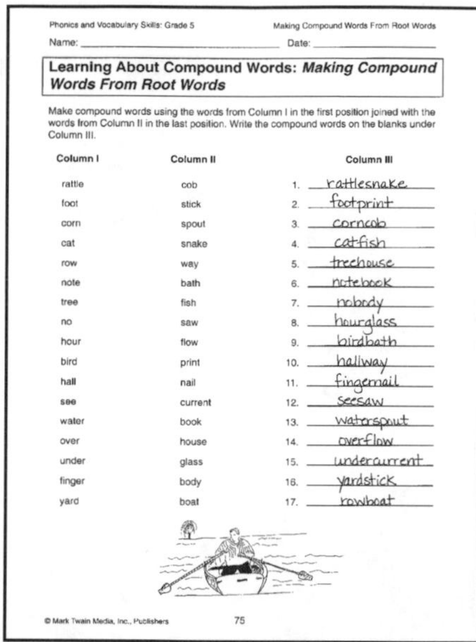

Phonics and Vocabulary Skills: Grade 5 — Making Compound Words From Root Words

Name: ____ Date: ____

Learning About Compound Words: *Making Compound Words From Root Words*

Make compound words using the words from Column I in the first position joined with the words from Column II in the last position. Write the compound words on the blanks under Column III.

Column I	Column II	Column III
rattle	cob	1. rattlesnake
foot	stick	2. footprint
corn	spout	3. corncob
cat	snake	4. catfish
row	way	5. treehouse
note	bath	6. notebook
tree	fish	7. nobody
no	saw	8. hourglass
hour	flow	9. birdbath
bird	print	10. hallway
hall	nail	11. fingernail
see	current	12. seesaw
water	book	13. waterspout
over	house	14. overflow
under	glass	15. undercurrent
finger	body	16. yardstick
yard	boat	17. rowboat

© Mark Twain Media, Inc., Publishers 75

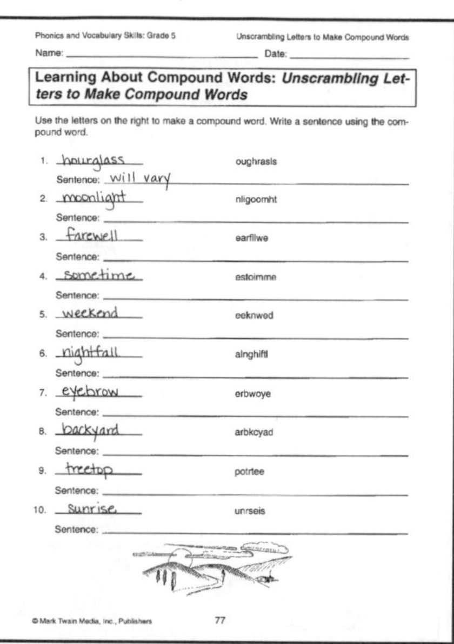

Phonics and Vocabulary Skills: Grade 5 — Unscrambling Letters to Make Compound Words

Name: ____ Date: ____

Learning About Compound Words: *Unscrambling Letters to Make Compound Words*

Use the letters on the right to make a compound word. Write a sentence using the compound word.

1. hourglass — oughrasls
   Sentence: will vary
2. moonlight — nligoomht
   Sentence:
3. farewell — earfllwe
   Sentence:
4. sometime — estoimme
   Sentence:
5. weekend — eeknwed
   Sentence:
6. nightfall — alnghiffl
   Sentence:
7. eyebrow — erbwoye
   Sentence:
8. backyard — arbkcyad
   Sentence:
9. treetop — potrtee
   Sentence:
10. sunrise — unrseis
   Sentence:

© Mark Twain Media, Inc., Publishers 77

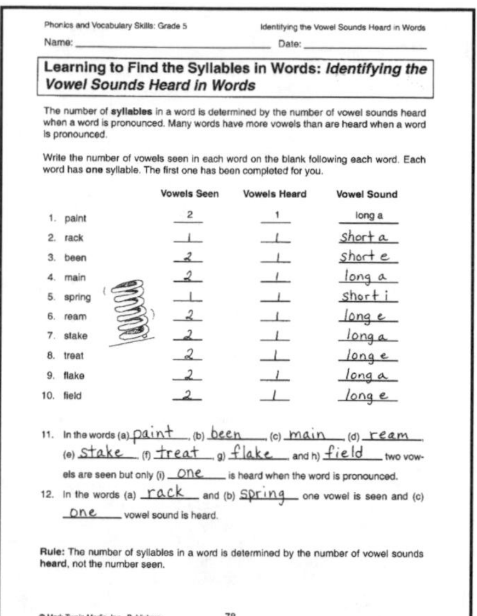

Phonics and Vocabulary Skills: Grade 5 — Identifying the Vowel Sounds Heard in Words

Name: ____ Date: ____

Learning to Find the Syllables in Words: *Identifying the Vowel Sounds Heard in Words*

The number of **syllables** in a word is determined by the number of vowel sounds heard when a word is pronounced. Many words have more vowels than are heard when a word is pronounced.

Write the number of vowels seen in each word on the blank following each word. Each word has **one** syllable. The first one has been completed for you.

Word	Vowels Seen	Vowels Heard	Vowel Sound
1. paint	2	1	long a
2. rack	1	1	short a
3. been	2	1	short e
4. main	2	1	long a
5. spring	1	1	short i
6. ream	2	1	long e
7. stake	2	1	long a
8. treat	2	1	long e
9. flake	2	1	long a
10. field	2	1	long e

11. In the words (a) paint, (b) been, (c) main, (d) ream, (e) stake, (f) treat, (g) flake, and (h) field two vowels are seen but only (i) one is heard when the word is pronounced.
12. In the words (a) rack and (b) spring one vowel is seen and (c) one vowel sound is heard.

Rule: The number of syllables in a word is determined by the number of vowel sounds **heard**, not the number **seen**.

© Mark Twain Media, Inc., Publishers 78

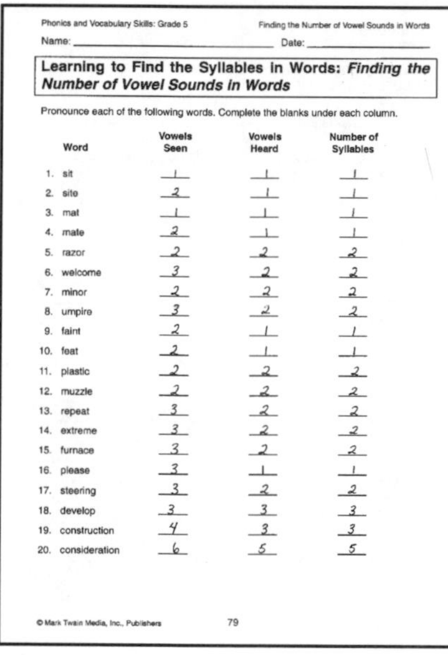

Phonics and Vocabulary Skills: Grade 5 — Finding the Number of Vowel Sounds in Words

Name: ____ Date: ____

Learning to Find the Syllables in Words: *Finding the Number of Vowel Sounds in Words*

Pronounce each of the following words. Complete the blanks under each column.

Word	Vowels Seen	Vowels Heard	Number of Syllables
1. sit	1	1	1
2. site	2	1	1
3. mat	1	1	1
4. mate	2	1	1
5. razor	2	2	2
6. welcome	3	2	2
7. minor	2	2	2
8. umpire	3	2	2
9. faint	2	1	1
10. feat	2	1	1
11. plastic	2	2	2
12. muzzle	2	2	2
13. repeat	3	2	2
14. extreme	3	2	2
15. furnace	3	2	2
16. please	3	1	1
17. steering	3	2	2
18. develop	3	3	3
19. construction	4	3	3
20. consideration	6	5	5

© Mark Twain Media, Inc., Publishers 79

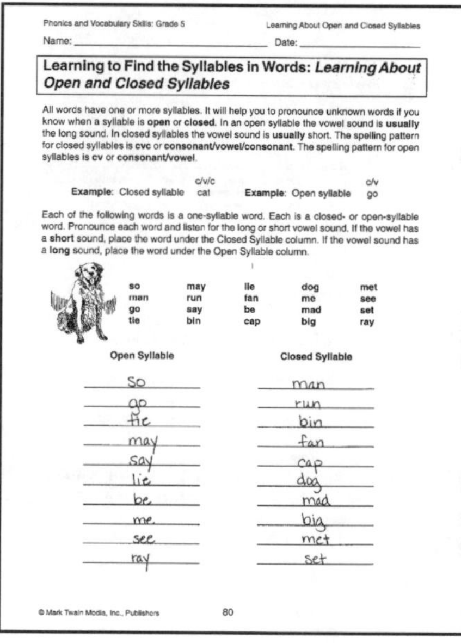

Phonics and Vocabulary Skills: Grade 5 — Learning About Open and Closed Syllables

Name: ____ Date: ____

Learning to Find the Syllables in Words: *Learning About Open and Closed Syllables*

All words have one or more syllables. It will help you to pronounce unknown words if you know when a syllable is **open** or **closed**. In an open syllable the vowel sound is **usually** the long sound. In closed syllables the vowel sound is **usually** short. The spelling pattern for closed syllables is **cvc** or **consonant/vowel/consonant**. The spelling pattern for open syllables is **cv** or **consonant/vowel**.

Example: Closed syllable c/v/c cat **Example:** Open syllable c/v go

Each of the following words is a one-syllable word. Each is a closed- or open-syllable word. Pronounce each word and listen for the long or short vowel sound. If the vowel has a **short** sound, place the word under the Closed Syllable column. If the vowel sound has a **long** sound, place the word under the Open Syllable column.

so	may	lie	dog	met
man	run	fan	me	see
go	say	be	mad	set
tie	bin	cap	big	ray

Open Syllable	Closed Syllable
so	man
go	run
tie	bin
may	fan
say	cap
lie	dog
be	mad
me	big
see	met
ray	set

© Mark Twain Media, Inc., Publishers 80

Phonics and Vocabulary Skills: Grade 5 — Finding the Syllables in Two-Syllable Words

Name: ____ Date: ____

Learning to Find the Syllables in Words: *Finding the Syllables in Two-Syllable Words*

When a two-syllable word is pronounced, two vowel sounds are heard.

Example: begin

When a word has a consonant between two vowels, the syllables are usually divided after the first vowel.

Example: be / gin The spelling pattern is cv/cvc (or cv/cv).

Divide each of the following words after the first vowel. Write the syllables on the blanks. Read the sentence that follows. The first one has been completed for you.

Word	1st Syllable	Vowel (long/short)	2nd Syllable	Vowel (long/short/silent/r-controlled)
1. bacon	ba	long	con	short
We had bacon for breakfast.				
2. below	be	long	low	long
The sailors went below deck.				
3. hobo	ho	long	bo	long
The hobo rode the train from city to city.				
4. hotel	ho	long	tel	short
We spent the evening at the hotel.				
5. local	lo	long	cal	short
Many local citizens were present.				
6. polite	po	long	lite	long
We were told to be polite.				
7. vapor	va	long	por	r-controlled
The jet plane left a vapor trail in the sky.				
8. delay	de	long	lay	long
It is important that we leave without delay.				
9. miser	mi	long	ser	r-controlled
The miser lived in a cave to save money.				
10. fatal	fa	long	tal	short
They made a fatal mistake that cost them the game.				

© Mark Twain Media, Inc., Publishers 81

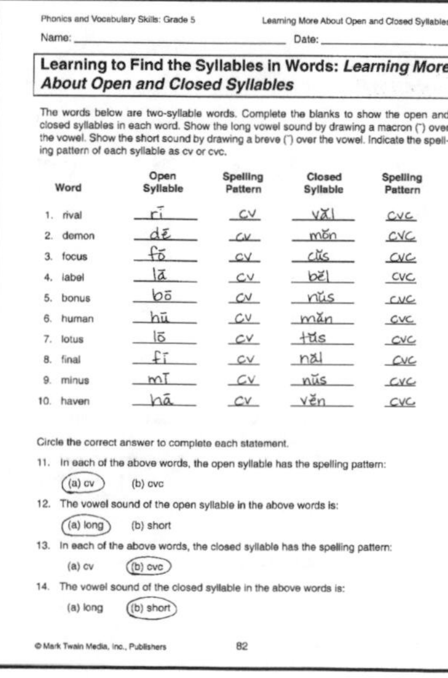

Phonics and Vocabulary Skills: Grade 5 — Learning More About Open and Closed Syllables

Name: ____ Date: ____

Learning to Find the Syllables in Words: *Learning More About Open and Closed Syllables*

The words below are two-syllable words. Complete the blanks to show the open and closed syllables in each word. Show the long vowel sound by drawing a macron (¯) over the vowel. Show the short sound by drawing a breve (˘) over the vowel. Indicate the spelling pattern of each syllable as cv or cvc.

Word	Open Syllable	Spelling Pattern	Closed Syllable	Spelling Pattern
1. rival	rī	cv	văl	cvc
2. demon	dē	cv	mŏn	cvc
3. focus	fō	cv	cŭs	cvc
4. label	lā	cv	bĕl	cvc
5. bonus	bō	cv	nŭs	cvc
6. human	hū	cv	măn	cvc
7. lotus	lō	cv	tŭs	cvc
8. final	fī	cv	năl	cvc
9. minus	mī	cv	nŭs	cvc
10. haven	hā	cv	vĕn	cvc

Circle the correct answer to complete each statement.

11. In each of the above words, the open syllable has the spelling pattern: **(a) cv** (b) cvc
12. The vowel sound of the open syllable in the above words is: **(a) long** (b) short
13. In each of the above words, the closed syllable has the spelling pattern: (a) cv **(b) cvc**
14. The vowel sound of the closed syllable in the above words is: (a) long **(b) short**

© Mark Twain Media, Inc., Publishers 82

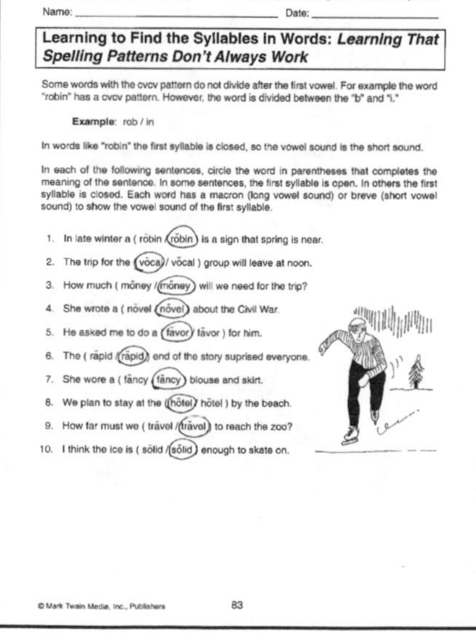

Phonics and Vocabulary Skills: Grade 5 — Learning That Spelling Patterns Don't Always Work

Name: ____ Date: ____

Learning to Find the Syllables in Words: *Learning That Spelling Patterns Don't Always Work*

Some words with the cvcv pattern do not divide after the first vowel. For example the word "robin" has a cvcv pattern. However, the word is divided between the "b" and "i."

Example: rob / in

In words like "robin" the first syllable is closed, so the vowel sound is the short sound.

In each of the following sentences, circle the word in parentheses that completes the meaning of the sentence. In some sentences, the first syllable is open. In others the first syllable is closed. Each word has a macron (long vowel sound) or breve (short vowel sound) to show the vowel sound of the first syllable.

1. In late winter a (rōbin / **rŏbin**) is a sign that spring is near.
2. The trip for the (**vōcal** / vŏcal) group will leave at noon.
3. How much (mōney / **mŏney**) will we need for the trip?
4. She wrote a (nōvel / **nŏvel**) about the Civil War.
5. He asked me to do a (**fāvor** / făvor) for him.
6. The (rāpid / **răpid**) end of the story suprised everyone.
7. She wore a (fāncy / **făncy**) blouse and skirt.
8. We plan to stay at the (**hōtel** / hŏtel) by the beach.
9. How far must we (trāvel / **trăvel**) to reach the zoo?
10. I think the ice is (sōlid / **sŏlid**) enough to skate on.

© Mark Twain Media, Inc., Publishers 83

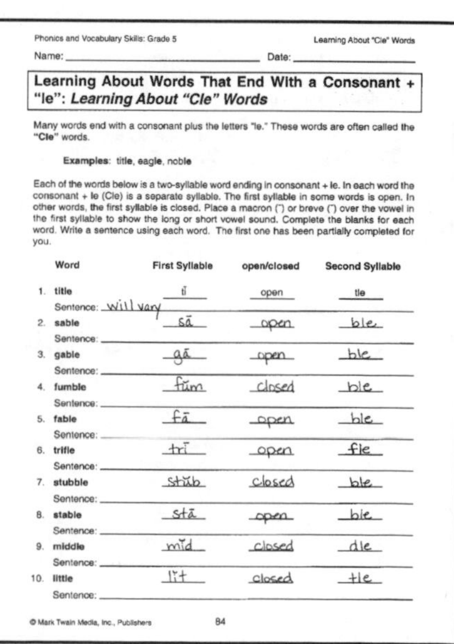

Phonics and Vocabulary Skills: Grade 5 — Learning About "Cle" Words

Name: ____ Date: ____

Learning About Words That End With a Consonant + "le": *Learning About "Cle" Words*

Many words end with a consonant plus the letters "le." These words are often called the **"Cle"** words.

Examples: title, eagle, noble

Each of the words below is a two-syllable word ending in consonant + le. In each word the consonant + le (Cle) is a separate syllable. The first syllable in some words is open. In other words, the first syllable is closed. Place a macron (¯) or breve (˘) over the vowel in the first syllable to show the long or short vowel sound. Complete the blanks for each word. Write a sentence using each word. The first one has been partially completed for you.

Word	First Syllable	open/closed	Second Syllable
1. title	tī	open	tle
Sentence: will vary			
2. sable	sā	open	ble
Sentence:			
3. gable	gā	open	ble
Sentence:			
4. fumble	fŭm	closed	ble
Sentence:			
5. fable	fā	open	ble
Sentence:			
6. trifle	trī	open	fle
Sentence:			
7. stubble	stŭb	closed	ble
Sentence:			
8. stable	stā	open	ble
Sentence:			
9. middle	mĭd	closed	dle
Sentence:			
10. little	lĭt	closed	tle
Sentence:			

© Mark Twain Media, Inc., Publishers 84

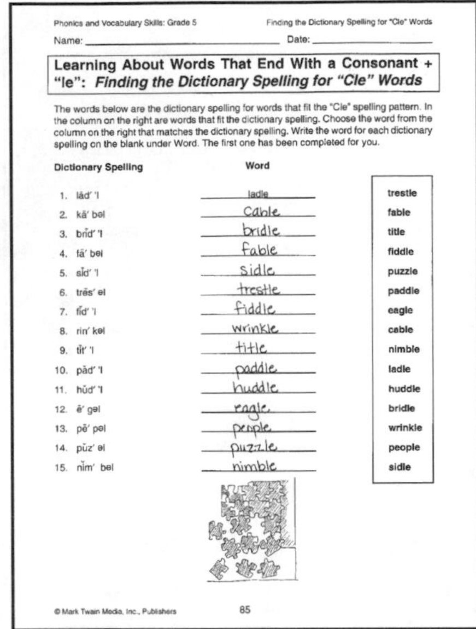

Phonics and Vocabulary Skills: Grade 5 — Finding the Dictionary Spelling for "Cle" Words

Name: ____ Date: ____

Learning About Words That End With a Consonant + "le": *Finding the Dictionary Spelling for "Cle" Words*

The words below are the dictionary spelling for words that fit the "Cle" spelling pattern. In the column on the right are words that fit the dictionary spelling. Choose the word from the column on the right that matches the dictionary spelling. Write the word for each dictionary spelling on the blank under Word. The first one has been completed for you.

	Dictionary Spelling	Word	
1.	lād' 'l	ladle	trestle
2.	kā' bəl	cable	fable
3.	brīd' 'l	bridle	title
4.	fā' bəl	fable	fiddle
5.	sīd' 'l	sidle	puzzle
6.	tres' əl	trestle	paddle
7.	fid' 'l	fiddle	eagle
8.	rin' kəl	wrinkle	cable
9.	tīt' 'l	title	nimble
10.	pad' 'l	paddle	ladle
11.	hud' 'l	huddle	huddle
12.	ē' gəl	eagle	bridle
13.	pē' pəl	people	wrinkle
14.	puz' əl	puzzle	people
15.	nim' bəl	nimble	sidle

© Mark Twain Media, Inc., Publishers 85

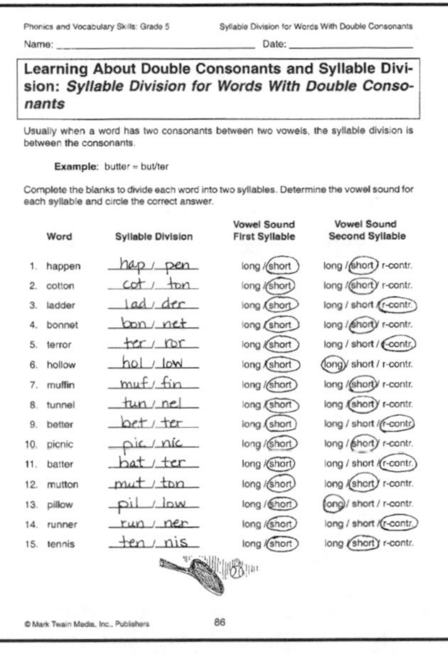

Phonics and Vocabulary Skills: Grade 5 — Syllable Division for Words With Double Consonants

Name: ____ Date: ____

Learning About Double Consonants and Syllable Division: *Syllable Division for Words With Double Consonants*

Usually when a word has two consonants between two vowels, the syllable division is between the consonants.

Example: butter = but/ter

Complete the blanks to divide each word into two syllables. Determine the vowel sound for each syllable and circle the correct answer.

	Word	Syllable Division	Vowel Sound First Syllable	Vowel Sound Second Syllable
1.	happen	hap / pen	short	short
2.	cotton	cot / ton	short	short
3.	ladder	lad / der	short	r-contr.
4.	bonnet	bon / net	short	short
5.	terror	ter / ror	short	r-contr.
6.	hollow	hol / low	short	long
7.	muffin	muf / fin	short	short
8.	tunnel	tun / nel	short	short
9.	better	bet / ter	short	r-contr.
10.	picnic	pic / nic	short	short
11.	batter	bat / ter	short	r-contr.
12.	mutton	mut / ton	short	short
13.	pillow	pil / low	short	long
14.	runner	run / ner	short	r-contr.
15.	tennis	ten / nis	short	short

© Mark Twain Media, Inc., Publishers 86

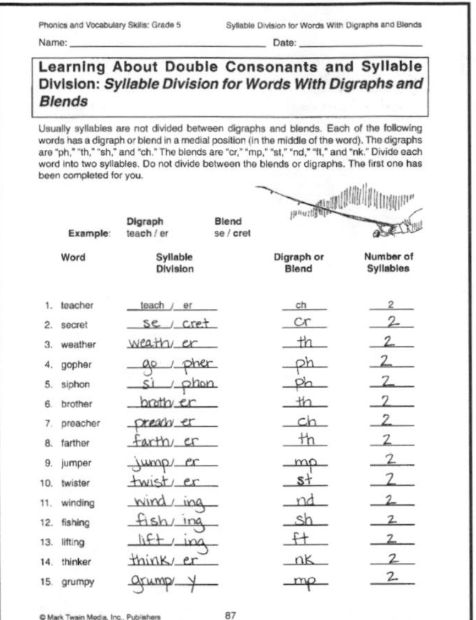

Phonics and Vocabulary Skills: Grade 5 — Syllable Division for Words With Digraphs and Blends

Name: ____ Date: ____

Learning About Double Consonants and Syllable Division: *Syllable Division for Words With Digraphs and Blends*

Usually syllables are not divided between digraphs and blends. Each of the following words has a digraph or blend in a medial position (in the middle of the word). The digraphs are "ph," "th," "sh," and "ch." The blends are "cr," "mp," "st," "nd," "ft," and "nk." Divide each word into two syllables. Do not divide between the blends or digraphs. The first one has been completed for you.

Example: Digraph teach / er; Blend se / cret

	Word	Syllable Division	Digraph or Blend	Number of Syllables
1.	teacher	teach / er	ch	2
2.	secret	se / cret	cr	2
3.	weather	weath / er	th	2
4.	gopher	go / pher	ph	2
5.	siphon	si / phon	ph	2
6.	brother	broth / er	th	2
7.	preacher	preach / er	ch	2
8.	farther	farth / er	th	2
9.	jumper	jump / er	mp	2
10.	twister	twist / er	st	2
11.	winding	wind / ing	nd	2
12.	fishing	fish / ing	sh	2
13.	lifting	lift / ing	ft	2
14.	thinker	think / er	nk	2
15.	grumpy	grump / y	mp	2

© Mark Twain Media, Inc., Publishers 87

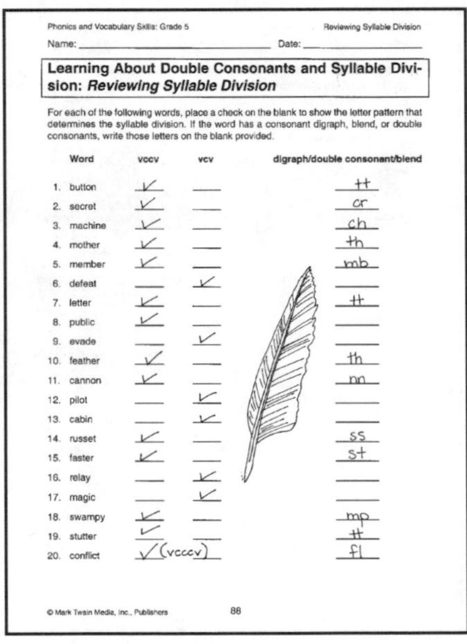

Phonics and Vocabulary Skills: Grade 5 — Reviewing Syllable Division

Name: ____ Date: ____

Learning About Double Consonants and Syllable Division: *Reviewing Syllable Division*

For each of the following words, place a check on the blank to show the letter pattern that determines the syllable division. If the word has a consonant digraph, blend, or double consonants, write those letters on the blank provided.

	Word	vccv	vcv	digraph/double consonant/blend
1.	button	✓		tt
2.	secret	✓		cr
3.	machine	✓		ch
4.	mother	✓		th
5.	member	✓		mb
6.	defeat		✓	
7.	letter	✓		tt
8.	public	✓		
9.	evade		✓	
10.	feather	✓		th
11.	cannon	✓		nn
12.	pilot		✓	
13.	cabin		✓	
14.	russet	✓		ss
15.	faster	✓		st
16.	relay		✓	
17.	magic		✓	
18.	swampy	✓		mp
19.	stutter	✓		tt
20.	conflict	✓ (vcccv)		fl

© Mark Twain Media, Inc., Publishers 88

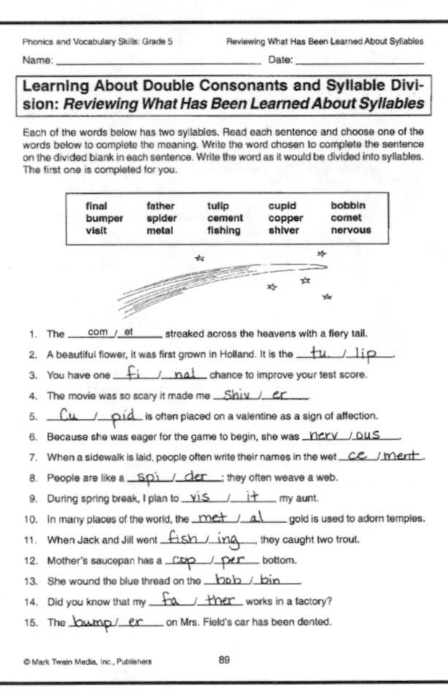

Phonics and Vocabulary Skills: Grade 5 — Reviewing What Has Been Learned About Syllables

Name: ____ Date: ____

Learning About Double Consonants and Syllable Division: *Reviewing What Has Been Learned About Syllables*

Each of the words below has two syllables. Read each sentence and choose one of the words below to complete the meaning. Write the word chosen to complete the sentence on the divided blank in each sentence. Write the word as it would be divided into syllables. The first one is completed for you.

final	father	tulip	cupid	bobbin
bumper	spider	cement	copper	comet
visit	metal	fishing	shiver	nervous

1. The com / et streaked across the heavens with a fiery tail.
2. A beautiful flower, it was first grown in Holland. It is the tu / lip.
3. You have one fi / nal chance to improve your test score.
4. The movie was so scary it made me shiv / er.
5. Cu / pid is often placed on a valentine as a sign of affection.
6. Because she was eager for the game to begin, she was nerv / ous.
7. When a sidewalk is laid, people often write their names in the wet ce / ment.
8. People are like a spi / der; they often weave a web.
9. During spring break, I plan to vis / it my aunt.
10. In many places of the world, the met / al gold is used to adorn temples.
11. When Jack and Jill went fish / ing, they caught two trout.
12. Mother's saucepan has a cop / per bottom.
13. She wound the blue thread on the bob / bin.
14. Did you know that my fa / ther works in a factory?
15. The bump / er on Mrs. Field's car has been dented.

© Mark Twain Media, Inc., Publishers 89

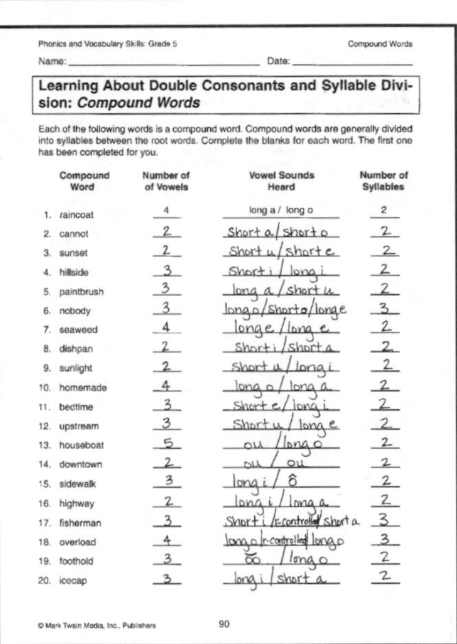

Phonics and Vocabulary Skills: Grade 5 — Compound Words

Name: ____ Date: ____

Learning About Double Consonants and Syllable Division: *Compound Words*

Each of the following words is a compound word. Compound words are generally divided into syllables between the root words. Complete the blanks for each word. The first one has been completed for you.

	Compound Word	Number of Vowels	Vowel Sounds Heard	Number of Syllables
1.	raincoat	4	long a / long o	2
2.	cannot	2	short a / short o	2
3.	sunset	2	short u / short e	2
4.	hillside	3	short i / long i	2
5.	paintbrush	3	long a / short u	2
6.	nobody	3	long o / short o / long e	3
7.	seaweed	4	long e / long e	2
8.	dishpan	2	short i / short a	2
9.	sunlight	2	short u / long i	2
10.	homemade	4	long o / long a	2
11.	bedtime	3	short e / long i	2
12.	upstream	3	short u / long e	2
13.	houseboat	5	ou / long o	2
14.	downtown	2	ou / ou	2
15.	sidewalk	3	long i / ô	2
16.	highway	2	long i / long a	2
17.	fisherman	3	short i / r-controlled / short a	3
18.	overload	4	long o / r-controlled / long o	3
19.	foothold	3	o͝o / long o	2
20.	icecap	3	long i / short a	2

© Mark Twain Media, Inc., Publishers 90

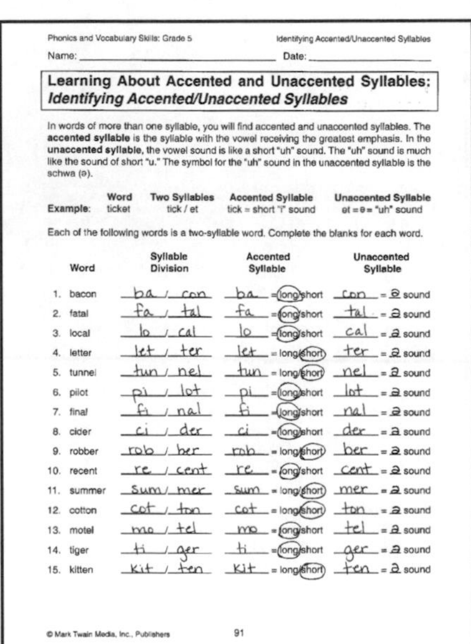

Phonics and Vocabulary Skills: Grade 5 — Identifying Accented/Unaccented Syllables

Name: ____ Date: ____

Learning About Accented and Unaccented Syllables: *Identifying Accented/Unaccented Syllables*

In words of more than one syllable, you will find accented and unaccented syllables. The **accented syllable** is the syllable with the vowel receiving the greatest emphasis. In the **unaccented syllable**, the vowel sound is like a short "uh" sound. The "uh" sound is much like the sound of short "u." The symbol for the "uh" sound in the unaccented syllable is the schwa (ə).

	Word	Two Syllables	Accented Syllable	Unaccented Syllable
Example:	ticket	tick / et	tick = short "i" sound	et = ə = "uh" sound

Each of the following words is a two-syllable word. Complete the blanks for each word.

	Word	Syllable Division	Accented Syllable	Unaccented Syllable
1.	bacon	ba / con	ba = long	con = ə sound
2.	fatal	fa / tal	fa = long	tal = ə sound
3.	local	lo / cal	lo = long	cal = ə sound
4.	letter	let / ter	let = short	ter = ə sound
5.	tunnel	tun / nel	tun = short	nel = ə sound
6.	pilot	pi / lot	pi = long	lot = ə sound
7.	final	fi / nal	fi = long	nal = ə sound
8.	cider	ci / der	ci = long	der = ə sound
9.	robber	rob / ber	rob = short	ber = ə sound
10.	recent	re / cent	re = long	cent = ə sound
11.	summer	sum / mer	sum = short	mer = ə sound
12.	cotton	cot / ton	cot = short	ton = ə sound
13.	motel	mo / tel	mo = long	tel = ə sound
14.	tiger	ti / ger	ti = long	ger = ə sound
15.	kitten	kit / ten	kit = short	ten = ə sound

© Mark Twain Media, Inc., Publishers 91

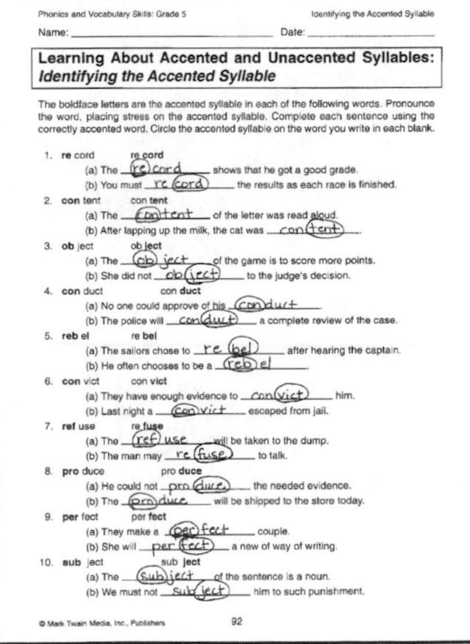

Phonics and Vocabulary Skills: Grade 5 — Identifying the Accented Syllable

Name: ____ Date: ____

Learning About Accented and Unaccented Syllables: *Identifying the Accented Syllable*

The boldface letters are the accented syllable in each of the following words. Pronounce the word, placing stress on the accented syllable. Complete each sentence using the correctly accented word. Circle the accented syllable on the word you write in each blank.

1. **re** cord — re **cord**
   (a) The (re)cord shows that he got a good grade.
   (b) You must re(cord) the results as each race is finished.
2. **con** tent — con **tent**
   (a) The (con)tent of the letter was read aloud.
   (b) After lapping up the milk, the cat was con(tent).
3. **ob** ject — ob **ject**
   (a) The (ob)ject of the game is to score more points.
   (b) She did not ob(ject) to the judge's decision.
4. **con** duct — con **duct**
   (a) No one could approve of his (con)duct.
   (b) The police will con(duct) a complete review of the case.
5. **reb** el — re **bel**
   (a) The sailors chose to re(bel) after hearing the captain.
   (b) He often chooses to be a (reb)el.
6. **con** vict — con **vict**
   (a) They have enough evidence to con(vict) him.
   (b) Last night a (con)vict escaped from jail.
7. **ref** use — re **fuse**
   (a) The (ref)use will be taken to the dump.
   (b) The man may re(fuse) to talk.
8. **pro** duce — pro **duce**
   (a) He could not pro(duce) the needed evidence.
   (b) The (pro)duce will be shipped to the store today.
9. **per** fect — per **fect**
   (a) They make a (per)fect couple.
   (b) She will per(fect) a new of way of writing.
10. **sub** ject — sub **ject**
    (a) The (sub)ject of the sentence is a noun.
    (b) We must not sub(ject) him to such punishment.

© Mark Twain Media, Inc., Publishers 92

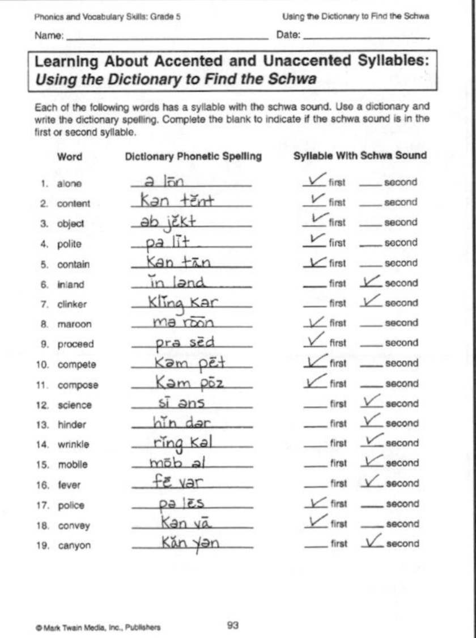

Phonics and Vocabulary Skills: Grade 5 — Using the Dictionary to Find the Schwa

Name: ____ Date: ____

Learning About Accented and Unaccented Syllables: *Using the Dictionary to Find the Schwa*

Each of the following words has a syllable with the schwa sound. Use a dictionary and write the dictionary spelling. Complete the blank to indicate if the schwa sound is in the first or second syllable.

	Word	Dictionary Phonetic Spelling	Syllable With Schwa Sound
1.	alone	ə lōn	✓ first
2.	content	kən tĕnt	✓ first
3.	object	əb jĕkt	✓ first
4.	polite	pə līt	✓ first
5.	contain	kən tān	✓ first
6.	inland	ĭn lənd	✓ second
7.	clinker	klĭng kər	✓ second
8.	maroon	mə rōōn	✓ first
9.	proceed	prə sēd	✓ first
10.	compete	kəm pēt	✓ first
11.	compose	kəm pōz	✓ first
12.	science	sī əns	✓ second
13.	hinder	hĭn dər	✓ second
14.	wrinkle	rĭng kəl	✓ second
15.	mobile	mōb əl	✓ second
16.	fever	fē vər	✓ second
17.	police	pə lēs	✓ first
18.	convey	kən vā	✓ first
19.	canyon	kăn yən	✓ second

© Mark Twain Media, Inc., Publishers 93

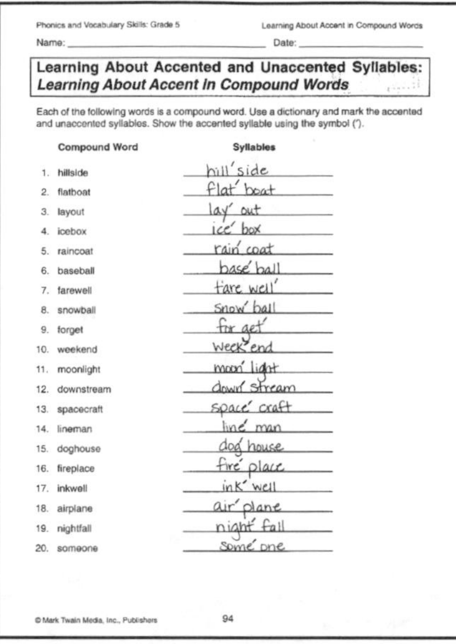

Phonics and Vocabulary Skills: Grade 5 Learning About Accent in Compound Words

Name: Date:

Learning About Accented and Unaccented Syllables: *Learning About Accent in Compound Words*

Each of the following words is a compound word. Use a dictionary and mark the accented and unaccented syllables. Show the accented syllable using the symbol (´).

Compound Word	Syllables
1. hillside	hill´ side
2. flatboat	flat´ boat
3. layout	lay´ out
4. icebox	ice´ box
5. raincoat	rain´ coat
6. baseball	base´ ball
7. farewell	fare well´
8. snowball	snow´ ball
9. forget	for get´
10. weekend	week´ end
11. moonlight	moon´ light
12. downstream	down´ stream
13. spacecraft	space´ craft
14. lineman	line´ man
15. doghouse	dog´ house
16. fireplace	fire´ place
17. inkwell	ink´ well
18. airplane	air´ plane
19. nightfall	night´ fall
20. someone	some´ one

© Mark Twain Media, Inc., Publishers 94

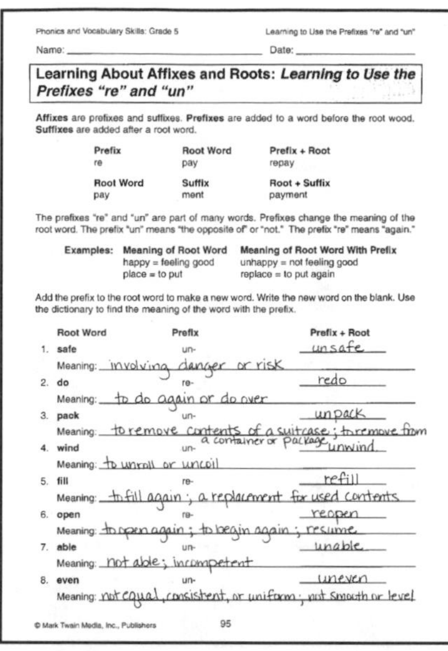

Phonics and Vocabulary Skills: Grade 5 Learning to Use the Prefixes "re" and "un"

Name: Date:

Learning About Affixes and Roots: *Learning to Use the Prefixes "re" and "un"*

Affixes are prefixes and suffixes. **Prefixes** are added to a word before the root word. **Suffixes** are added after a root word.

Prefix	Root Word	Prefix + Root
re	pay	repay

Root Word	Suffix	Root + Suffix
pay	ment	payment

The prefixes "re" and "un" are part of many words. Prefixes change the meaning of the root word. The prefix "un" means "the opposite of" or "not." The prefix "re" means "again."

Examples: **Meaning of Root Word** happy = feeling good; place = to put. **Meaning of Root Word With Prefix** unhappy = not feeling good; replace = to put again

Add the prefix to the root word to make a new word. Write the new word on the blank. Use the dictionary to find the meaning of the word with the prefix.

Root Word	Prefix	Prefix + Root
1. safe	un-	unsafe
2. do	re-	redo
3. pack	un-	unpack
4. wind	un-	unwind
5. fill	re-	refill
6. open	re-	reopen
7. able	un-	unable
8. even	un-	uneven

1. Meaning: involving danger or risk
2. Meaning: to do again or do over
3. Meaning: to remove contents of a suitcase; to remove from a container or package
4. Meaning: to unroll or uncoil
5. Meaning: to fill again; a replacement for used contents
6. Meaning: to open again; to begin again; resume
7. Meaning: not able; incompetent
8. Meaning: not equal, consistent, or uniform; not smooth or level

© Mark Twain Media, Inc., Publishers 95

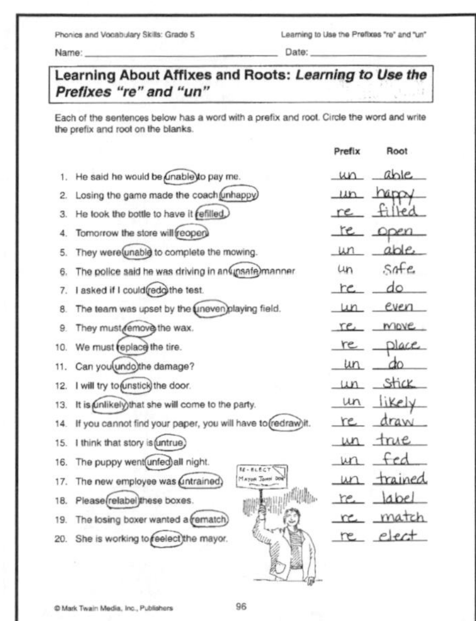

Phonics and Vocabulary Skills: Grade 5 Learning to Use the Prefixes "re" and "un"

Name: Date:

Learning About Affixes and Roots: *Learning to Use the Prefixes "re" and "un"*

Each of the sentences below has a word with a prefix and root. Circle the word and write the prefix and root on the blanks.

Sentence	Prefix	Root
1. He said he would be unable to pay me.	un	able
2. Losing the game made the coach unhappy.	un	happy
3. He took the bottle to have it refilled.	re	filled
4. Tomorrow the store will reopen.	re	open
5. They were unable to complete the mowing.	un	able
6. The police said he was driving in an unsafe manner.	un	safe
7. I asked if I could redo the test.	re	do
8. The team was upset by the uneven playing field.	un	even
9. They must remove the wax.	re	move
10. We must replace the tire.	re	place
11. Can you undo the damage?	un	do
12. I will try to unstick the door.	un	stick
13. It is unlikely that she will come to the party.	un	likely
14. If you cannot find your paper, you will have to redraw it.	re	draw
15. I think that story is untrue.	un	true
16. The puppy went unfed all night.	un	fed
17. The new employee was untrained.	un	trained
18. Please relabel these boxes.	re	label
19. The losing boxer wanted a rematch.	re	match
20. She is working to reelect the mayor.	re	elect

© Mark Twain Media, Inc., Publishers 96

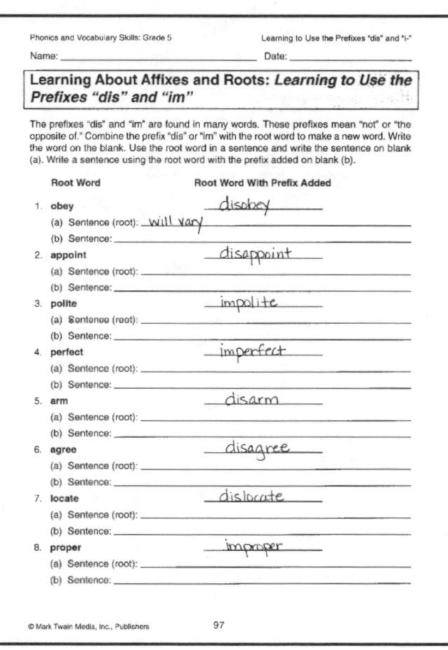

Phonics and Vocabulary Skills: Grade 5 Learning to Use the Prefixes "dis" and "im"

Name: Date:

Learning About Affixes and Roots: *Learning to Use the Prefixes "dis" and "im"*

The prefixes "dis" and "im" are found in many words. These prefixes mean "not" or "the opposite of." Combine the prefix "dis" or "im" with the root word to make a new word. Write the word on the blank. Use the root word in a sentence and write the sentence on blank (a). Write a sentence using the root word with the prefix added on blank (b).

Root Word	Root Word With Prefix Added
1. obey	disobey
2. appoint	disappoint
3. polite	impolite
4. perfect	imperfect
5. arm	disarm
6. agree	disagree
7. locate	dislocate
8. proper	improper

(a) Sentence (root): will vary

(b) Sentence:

© Mark Twain Media, Inc., Publishers 97

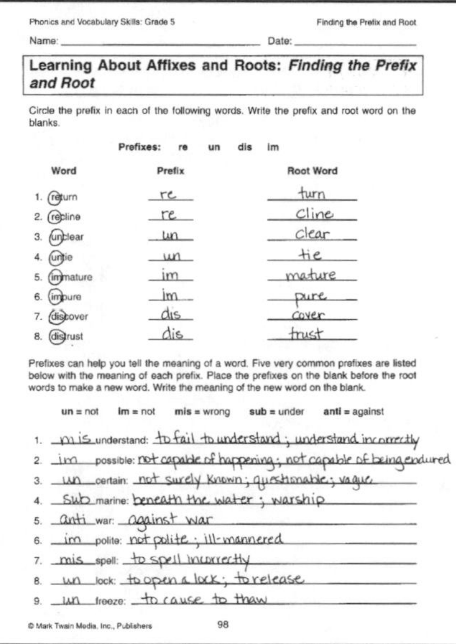

Phonics and Vocabulary Skills: Grade 5 Finding the Prefix and Root

Name: Date:

Learning About Affixes and Roots: *Finding the Prefix and Root*

Circle the prefix in each of the following words. Write the prefix and root word on the blanks.

Prefixes: re un dis im

Word	Prefix	Root Word
1. return	re	turn
2. recline	re	cline
3. unclear	un	clear
4. untie	un	tie
5. immature	im	mature
6. impure	im	pure
7. discover	dis	cover
8. distrust	dis	trust

Prefixes can help you tell the meaning of a word. Five very common prefixes are listed below with the meaning of each prefix. Place the prefixes on the blank before the root words to make a new word. Write the meaning of the new word on the blank.

un = not im = not mis = wrong sub = under anti = against

1. mis understand: to fail to understand; understand incorrectly
2. im possible: not capable of happening; not capable of being endured
3. un certain: not surely known; questionable; vague
4. sub marine: beneath the water; warship
5. anti war: against war
6. im polite: not polite; ill-mannered
7. mis spell: to spell incorrectly
8. un lock: to open a lock; to release
9. un freeze: to cause to thaw

© Mark Twain Media, Inc., Publishers 98

Phonics and Vocabulary Skills: Grade 5 Learning to Use the Suffixes "ful," "less," and "ly"

Name: Date:

Learning About Affixes and Roots: *Learning to Use the Suffixes "ful," "less," and "ly"*

Many words are made from a root with a suffix added.

Example: The root word "**care**" with the suffix "**ful**" becomes a new word: **careful**.

Add the suffix "ful," "less," or "ly" to the root words below to make a new word. Write the suffix on the first blank. Then write the new word on the second blank. Use a dictionary to find the meaning of the word with the suffix. Write a sentence using the word with the suffix.

Possible answers include:

Root Word	Suffix	Root + Suffix
1. care	less	careless
2. help	ful	helpful
3. hope	less	hopeless
4. sad	ly	sadly
5. kind	ly	kindly
6. man	ly	manly

1. Meaning: negligent; lack of thought; inconsiderate. Sentence: will vary
2. Meaning: providing help; useful; beneficial
3. Meaning: having no hope; despairing; impossible
4. Meaning: sorrowful; unhappy
5. Meaning: showing sympathy, considerateness, or helpfulness
6. Meaning: having the admirable qualities attributed to a man

© Mark Twain Media, Inc., Publishers 99

Phonics and Vocabulary Skills: Grade 5 Learning to Use the Suffixes "ful," "less," and "ly"

Name: Date:

Learning About Affixes and Roots: *Learning to Use the Suffixes "ful," "less," and "ly"*

Add the suffix "ful," "less," or "ly" to the root words below to make a new word. Write the suffix on the first blank. Then write the new word on the second blank. Use a dictionary to find the meaning of the word with the suffix. Write a sentence using the word with the suffix.

Possible answers include:

Root Word	Suffix	Root + Suffix
1. pain	less	painless
2. play	ful	playful
3. cheer	ful	cheerful
4. use	less	useless
5. bad	ly	badly
6. loud	ly	loudly

1. Meaning: free from pain
2. Meaning: full of fun; humorous; jesting
3. Meaning: in good spirits; promoting cheer
4. Meaning: having no beneficial purpose or use; of little or no worth
5. Meaning: not good; having undesirable qualities; unfavorable
6. Meaning: characterized by high volume and intensity of sound

© Mark Twain Media, Inc., Publishers 100

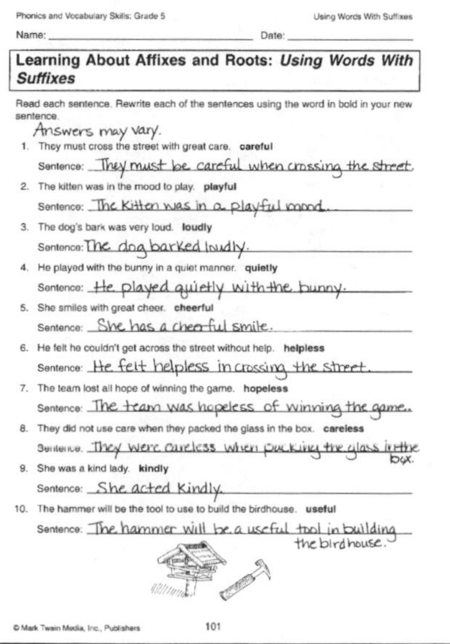

Phonics and Vocabulary Skills: Grade 5 Using Words With Suffixes

Name: Date:

Learning About Affixes and Roots: *Using Words With Suffixes*

Read each sentence. Rewrite each of the sentences using the word in bold in your new sentence.

Answers may vary.

1. They must cross the street with great care. **careful** Sentence: They must be careful when crossing the street.
2. The kitten was in the mood to play. **playful** Sentence: The kitten was in a playful mood.
3. The dog's bark was very loud. **loudly** Sentence: The dog barked loudly.
4. He played with the bunny in a quiet manner. **quietly** Sentence: He played quietly with the bunny.
5. She smiles with great cheer. **cheerful** Sentence: She has a cheerful smile.
6. He felt he couldn't get across the street without help. **helpless** Sentence: He felt helpless in crossing the street.
7. The team lost all hope of winning the game. **hopeless** Sentence: The team was hopeless of winning the game.
8. They did not use care when they packed the glass in the box. **careless** Sentence: They were careless when packing the glass in the box.
9. She was a kind lady. **kindly** Sentence: She acted kindly.
10. The hammer will be the tool to use to build the birdhouse. **useful** Sentence: The hammer will be a useful tool in building the birdhouse.

© Mark Twain Media, Inc., Publishers 101

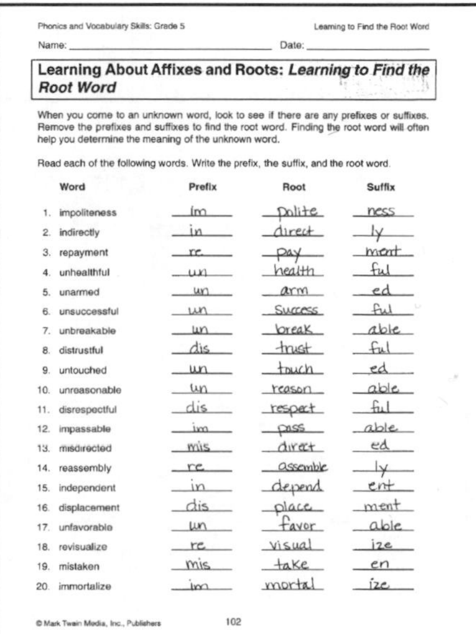

Phonics and Vocabulary Skills: Grade 5 Learning to Find the Root Word

Name: Date:

Learning About Affixes and Roots: *Learning to Find the Root Word*

When you come to an unknown word, look to see if there are any prefixes or suffixes. Remove the prefixes and suffixes to find the root word. Finding the root word will often help you determine the meaning of the unknown word.

Read each of the following words. Write the prefix, the suffix, and the root word.

Word	Prefix	Root	Suffix
1. impoliteness	im	polite	ness
2. indirectly	in	direct	ly
3. repayment	re	pay	ment
4. unhealthful	un	health	ful
5. unarmed	un	arm	ed
6. unsuccessful	un	success	ful
7. unbreakable	un	break	able
8. distrustful	dis	trust	ful
9. untouched	un	touch	ed
10. unreasonable	un	reason	able
11. disrespectful	dis	respect	ful
12. impassable	im	pass	able
13. misdirected	mis	direct	ed
14. reassembly	re	assemble	ly
15. independent	in	depend	ent
16. displacement	dis	place	ment
17. unfavorable	un	favor	able
18. revisualize	re	visual	ize
19. mistaken	mis	take	en
20. immortalize	im	mortal	ize

© Mark Twain Media, Inc., Publishers 102

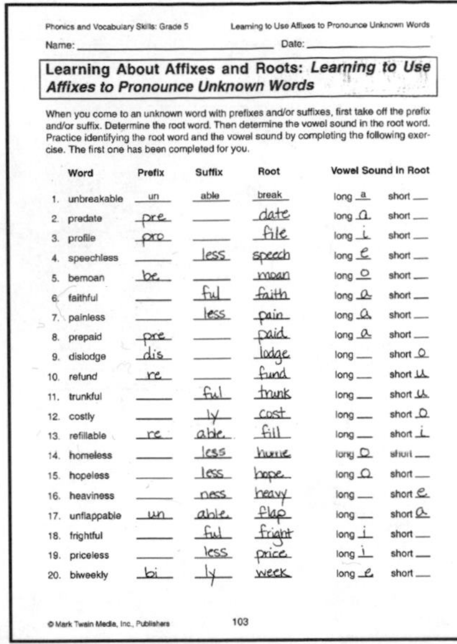
Phonics and Vocabulary Skills: Grade 5 Learning to Use Affixes to Pronounce Unknown Words

Name: ______ Date: ______

Learning About Affixes and Roots: ***Learning to Use Affixes to Pronounce Unknown Words***

When you come to an unknown word with prefixes and/or suffixes, first take off the prefix and/or suffix. Determine the root word. Then determine the vowel sound in the root word. Practice identifying the root word and the vowel sound by completing the following exercise. The first one has been completed for you.

	Word	Prefix	Suffix	Root	Vowel Sound in Root: long	short
1.	unbreakable	un	able	break	a	
2.	predate	pre		date	a	
3.	profile	pro		file	i	
4.	speechless		less	speech	e	
5.	bemoan	be		moan	o	
6.	faithful		ful	faith	a	
7.	painless		less	pain	a	
8.	prepaid	pre		paid	a	
9.	dislodge	dis		lodge		o
10.	refund	re		fund		u
11.	trunkful		ful	trunk		u
12.	costly		ly	cost		o
13.	refillable	re	able	fill		i
14.	homeless		less	home	o	
15.	hopeless		less	hope	o	
16.	heaviness		ness	heavy		e
17.	unflappable	un	able	flap		a
18.	frightful		ful	fright	i	
19.	priceless		less	price	i	
20.	biweekly	bi	ly	week	e	

© Mark Twain Media, Inc., Publishers 103

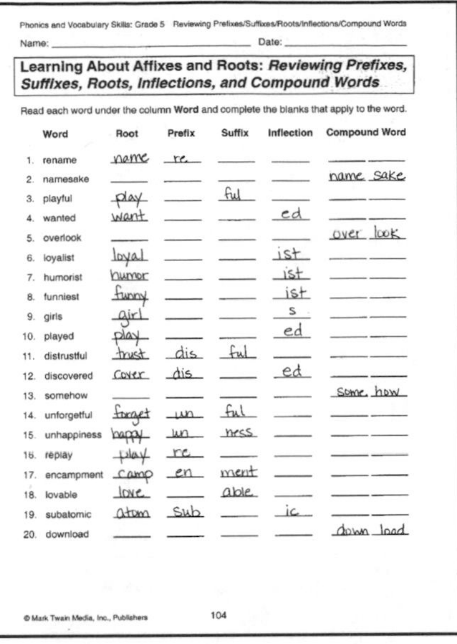
Phonics and Vocabulary Skills: Grade 5 Reviewing Prefixes/Suffixes/Roots/Inflections/Compound Words

Name: ______ Date: ______

Learning About Affixes and Roots: ***Reviewing Prefixes, Suffixes, Roots, Inflections, and Compound Words***

Read each word under the column **Word** and complete the blanks that apply to the word.

	Word	Root	Prefix	Suffix	Inflection	Compound Word
1.	rename	name	re			
2.	namesake					name sake
3.	playful	play		ful		
4.	wanted	want			ed	
5.	overlook					over look
6.	loyalist	loyal			ist	
7.	humorist	humor			ist	
8.	funniest	funny			ist	
9.	girls	girl			s	
10.	played	play			ed	
11.	distrustful	trust	dis	ful		
12.	discovered	cover	dis		ed	
13.	somehow					some how
14.	unforgetful	forget	un	ful		
15.	unhappiness	happy	un	ness		
16.	replay	play	re			
17.	encampment	camp	en	ment		
18.	lovable	love		able		
19.	subatomic	atom	sub		ic	
20.	download					down load

© Mark Twain Media, Inc., Publishers 104

Phonics and Vocabulary Skills: Grade 5 Learning About Antonyms

Name: ______ Date: ______

Learning About Antonyms, Synonyms, and Homonyms: ***Learning About Antonyms***

Antonyms are words that have opposite meanings.

Example: **big** and **small** are antonyms; these words are opposite in meaning.

On the right side of the page is a list of words that are antonyms for words in Column I. Write the word on the blank under Column II that means the opposite of the word in Column I.

	Column I	Column II	Word list
1.	hard	soft	sad
2.	small	large	dull
3.	hot	cold	enemy
4.	noisy	quiet	near
5.	buy	sell	remember
6.	above	below	bumpy
7.	day	night	die
8.	even	bumpy	open
9.	bright	dull	quiet
10.	empty	full	below
11.	cry	laugh	sell
12.	happy	sad	night
13.	close	open	soft
14.	far	near	cold
15.	forget	remember	captive
16.	complex	simple	laugh
17.	live	die	full
18.	free	captive	large
19.	friend	enemy	simple
20.	up	down	down

© Mark Twain Media, Inc., Publishers 105

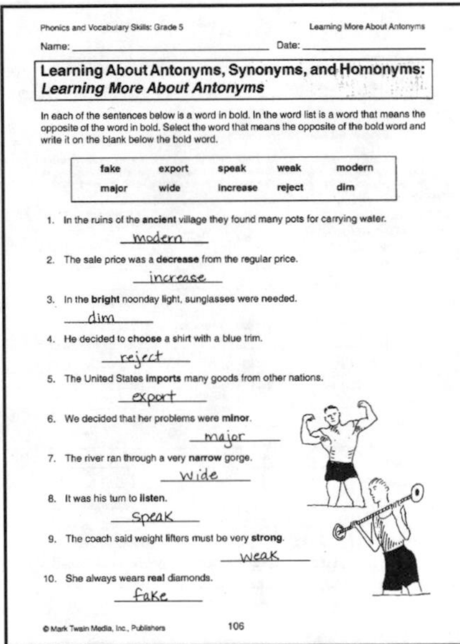
Phonics and Vocabulary Skills: Grade 5 Learning More About Antonyms

Name: ______ Date: ______

Learning About Antonyms, Synonyms, and Homonyms: ***Learning More About Antonyms***

In each of the sentences below is a word in bold. In the word list is a word that means the opposite of the word in bold. Select the word that means the opposite of the bold word and write it on the blank below the bold word.

fake	export	speak	weak	modern
major	wide	increase	reject	dim

1. In the ruins of the **ancient** village they found many pots for carrying water. modern
2. The sale price was a **decrease** from the regular price. increase
3. In the **bright** noonday light, sunglasses were needed. dim
4. He decided to **choose** a shirt with a blue trim. reject
5. The United States **imports** many goods from other nations. export
6. We decided that her problems were **minor**. major
7. The river ran through a very **narrow** gorge. wide
8. It was his turn to **listen**. speak
9. The coach said weight lifters must be very **strong**. weak
10. She always wears **real** diamonds. fake

© Mark Twain Media, Inc., Publishers 106

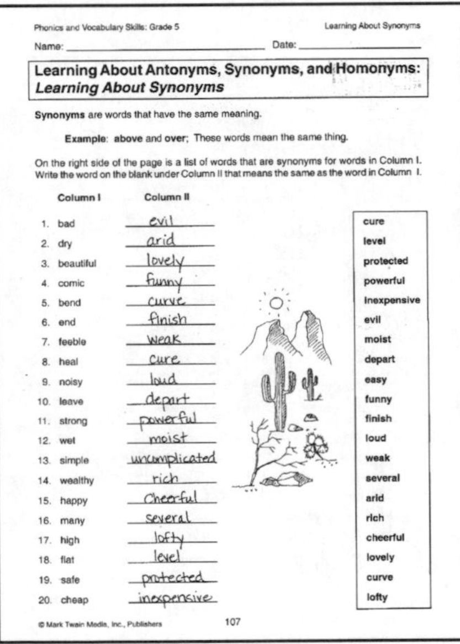
Phonics and Vocabulary Skills: Grade 5 Learning About Synonyms

Name: ______ Date: ______

Learning About Antonyms, Synonyms, and Homonyms: ***Learning About Synonyms***

Synonyms are words that have the same meaning.

Example: **above** and **over**; These words mean the same thing.

On the right side of the page is a list of words that are synonyms for words in Column I. Write the word on the blank under Column II that means the same as the word in Column I.

	Column I	Column II	Word list
1.	bad	evil	cure
2.	dry	arid	level
3.	beautiful	lovely	protected
4.	comic	funny	powerful
5.	bend	curve	inexpensive
6.	end	finish	evil
7.	feeble	weak	moist
8.	heal	cure	depart
9.	noisy	loud	easy
10.	leave	depart	funny
11.	strong	powerful	finish
12.	wet	moist	loud
13.	simple	uncomplicated	weak
14.	wealthy	rich	several
15.	happy	cheerful	arid
16.	many	several	rich
17.	high	lofty	cheerful
18.	flat	level	lovely
19.	safe	protected	curve
20.	cheap	inexpensive	lofty

© Mark Twain Media, Inc., Publishers 107

Phonics and Vocabulary Skills: Grade 5 Finding Synonyms

Name: ______ Date: ______

Learning About Antonyms, Synonyms, and Homonyms: ***Finding Synonyms***

In each of the sentences below is a word in bold. In the word list is a word that means the same as the word in bold. Select the word that means the same as the bold word and write it on the blank below the bold word.

reduced	brilliant	talk	actual	powerful
petty	thin	select	sends	old

1. In the ruins of the **ancient** village they found many pots for carrying water. old
2. The sale price had been **decreased** from the regular price. reduced
3. In the **bright** noonday light sunglasses were needed. brilliant
4. He decided to **choose** a shirt with a blue trim. select
5. The United States **exports** many goods to other nations. sends
6. They had a **minor** disagreement. petty
7. The river ran like a **narrow** line through the gorge. thin
8. It was his turn to **speak**. talk
9. The coach said weight lifters must be very **strong**. powerful
10. She always wears **real** diamonds. actual

© Mark Twain Media, Inc., Publishers 108

Phonics and Vocabulary Skills: Grade 5 Learning About Homonyms

Name: ______ Date: ______

Learning About Antonyms, Synonyms, and Homonyms: ***Learning About Homonyms***

Homonyms are two or more words that have the same pronunciation but are spelled differently and have different meanings.

Example: **buy** and **by**

The words in the word list below are homonyms for the words in Column I. Write the word on the blank under Column II that is a homonym for the word in Column I. Then use both homonyms in a sentence.

eight site week toe to four their inn fair heel hour sole

	Column I	Column II
1.	there	their
	Sentence: will vary	
2.	two	to
	Sentence:	
3.	for	four
	Sentence:	
4.	our	hour
	Sentence:	
5.	ate	eight
	Sentence:	
6.	tow	toe
	Sentence:	
7.	sight	site
	Sentence:	
8.	soul	sole
	Sentence:	
9.	weak	week
	Sentence:	
10.	in	inn
	Sentence:	

© Mark Twain Media, Inc., Publishers 109

Phonics and Vocabulary Skills: Grade 5 Using the Correct Homonyms

Name: ______ Date: ______

Learning About Antonyms, Synonyms, and Homonyms: ***Using the Correct Homonyms***

Read each of the following sentences and complete the blank using the correct homonym.

1. **isle aisle**
   (a) They walked down the aisle and sat in the front row.
   (b) They were planning a vacation on a small isle in the Atlantic Ocean.
2. **great grate**
   (a) The last play of the game was great.
   (b) Before lighting the grill, you must clean the grate.
3. **fair fare**
   (a) The fare for riding the ferry is twenty-five cents.
   (b) She decided that the teacher had been fair when grading the test.
4. **dew due**
   (a) The grass was wet from dew, so we could not mow the lawn.
   (b) I understood the bill was due on the first of each month.
5. **cereal serial**
   (a) They always eat cereal for breakfast.
   (b) To order the new part we will need the serial number.
6. **foul fowl**
   (a) A duck is an example of a fowl.
   (b) She caught the foul ball for the third out.
7. **pain pane**
   (a) When the ball hit the pane, it broke.
   (b) He was in great pain after falling from the ladder.
8. **sent scent**
   (a) Many animals leave a scent to mark their territory.
   (b) I sent the letter yesterday.
9. **beach beech**
   (a) We decided to go to the beach for vacation.
   (b) They sat beneath a beech tree and finished their homework.
10. **groan grown**
    (a) When he read the letter, we heard a loud groan.
    (b) His father did not have a car until he was grown.

S/N: WTR317984M

CEREAL

© Mark Twain Media, Inc., Publishers 110